HOW TO TALK TO ANYONE

IN A DIGITAL AGE

A Quickstart Guide to Gain Confidence,
Improve Social Skills, Overcome Shyness,
and Build Meaningful Connections

ROSHEL WAITE

FREE Bonus Gift #1

Scan the QR code for exclusive access to the FREE Resource Library!

FREE Bonus Gift #2

Scan the QR code to get a PDF copy of the Book for FREE!

To my incredible supporters,

Thank you for believing in me, even when I doubted myself. Your unwavering encouragement, love, and support have been the foundation of my journey. You've celebrated my victories, no matter how small, and lifted me up during my darkest moments. Your faith in my abilities has been my driving force.

To my critics and adversaries,

Thank you for challenging me and pushing me beyond my limits. Your doubts and criticisms have fueled my determination and resilience. You've taught me the invaluable lesson that adversity is not a setback, but a setup for a comeback. Your opposition has sharpened my focus and strengthened my resolve, proving that I can rise above any obstacle.

To everyone who has crossed my path,

You've all contributed to my growth in ways you might not even realize. Whether you offered a kind word or a harsh critique, you've played a part in my story. For that, I am profoundly grateful.

With deepest appreciation and respect. Thank you for being part of my story.

Contents

IMPORTANT - READ THIS FIRST!

Hey there, Friend!

Have you ever found yourself stuck in the corner of a crowded room—heart pounding, palms sweaty—desperately searching for something, *anything*, to say? Or maybe you've stared at your phone for way too long, rewriting the same text over and over, wondering if it sounds awkward, fake... or worse, gets completely ignored?

We live in a world buzzing with constant chatter, yet somehow, *real* connection feels harder than ever.

Here's the truth:

Digital communication promised to make things easier—but often, it leaves us feeling more anxious, isolated, and misunderstood. Research shows that many young adults experience high levels of anxiety when interacting with new people or even sending simple messages, despite spending hours each day on social media.

We're more connected than ever, yet lonelier than we've ever been.

I get it—**I've been there.**

I'm **Roshel Waite,** and as an ambivert—someone who's wrestled with both introverted fears and extroverted frustration—I've experienced the full spectrum of social struggles firsthand. I know what it feels like to not fit in, to panic in silence, to feel drained after small talk that doesn't go anywhere.

Through my website <https://roshelinarush.com> I've helped countless young adults navigate personal growth, financial freedom, and the art of confident connection. Now, I'm bringing that guidance directly to you.

Welcome to *How to Talk to Anyone in a Digital Age*

A Quickstart Guide to Gain Confidence, Improve Social Skills, Overcome Shyness, and Build Meaningful Connections

What makes this book different?

This isn't another vague list of tips and tricks. It's a **survival** guide—packed with **real-world strategies** and **practical exercises** designed specifically for the challenges of modern communication. Whether you're speaking face-to-face, texting, DMing, or Zooming, you'll discover how to show up with clarity, confidence, and compassion.

You'll learn how to:

- Tap into your authentic self and stop overthinking social interactions

- Adapt to different communication styles without losing your voice

- Overcome anxiety and navigate conversations with confidence

- Master empathy, cultural competence, and digital boundaries

- Build genuine connections—online and offline—that actually last

But here's the catch:

True transformation takes work. You have to commit—to the exercises, to the reflection, to showing up for yourself. If you do? You won't just talk differently—you'll *connect* differently. And that changes everything.

Grab Your Free Bonuses

I've created a **free digital resource library** filled with worksheets, checklists, and bonus tools to support your growth.

Just head to: roshelinarush.com/free-resource-library
Enter your name and email to get instant access—whether you bought this book or not.

So, are you ready to break free from social anxiety, step out of isolation, and unlock the power of meaningful communication?

Your journey starts here. Let's begin.

The Communication Blueprint - Why It's a Skill, Not a Superpower

"What you think, you become. What you feel, you attract. What you imagine, you create."

- Buddha

Have you ever noticed someone who walks into a room and instantly commands attention? They seem to have this magnetic presence, effortlessly engaging everyone around them. It's easy to assume that such charisma is an innate gift. I used to think that too. But here's the truth: effective communication isn't a talent you're born with—it's a skill you can develop.

In this chapter, we'll debunk common myths about communication, help you understand your unique communication style, and introduce practical strategies to enhance your interactions. Whether you're chatting with friends, participating in class discussions, or navigating digital conversations or in-person conversations, these insights will set the stage for meaningful connections.

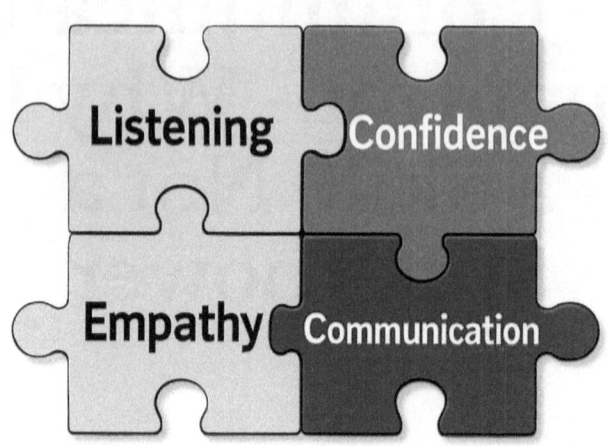

Debunking Communication Myths

Myth 1: Charisma Is Innate

I used to dread public speaking. My palms would sweat, my voice would shake, and afterward, I'd replay everything in my head, regretting what I did—or didn't—say. I believed charismatic people were born with something I lacked. But then I read about Winston Churchill. Despite his iconic speeches, he rehearsed obsessively (Lehrman, 2010). Charisma isn't magical—it's practiced.

That realization was huge. It gave me permission to show up imperfectly, knowing every conversation is practice for the next. Like building muscle, communication confidence is strengthened with repetition, not perfection.

Myth 2: One-Size-Fits-All Communication

Ever talk to someone and feel like they're just waiting for their turn to speak? That's passive listening. True listening is active. It requires focus, curiosity, and presence.

When someone really listens—leaning in, nodding, asking thoughtful questions—it changes the entire vibe of a conversation. Research shows active listening improves trust and relationship quality (Bodie, Worthington & Gearhart, 2013). It's not just what you hear—it's how you respond. I'll never forget how heard and seen I felt the first time a mentor listened to me like that. It's a habit I've worked to pass on ever since.

Myth 3: Listening Is Passive

Contrary to popular belief, listening is not a passive act—it's an active, intentional process that deeply engages your cognitive and emotional capacities. If you've ever spoken to someone who truly listened—someone who made you feel heard—you know it felt amazing. But it's easy to underestimate the effort that goes into genuine listening. Active listening isn't passive; it's fully engaged. You notice not just words but also emotions, tone, and body language.

Research (by Bodie, Worthington, & Gearhart, 2013) consistently shows that active listening dramatically improves interpersonal relationships, enhancing trust and mutual understanding. Becoming an active listener transforms superficial exchanges into meaningful interactions. I vividly remember a mentor who would lean forward, nodding as I spoke, genuinely curious. Their active listening made me feel valued and understood, a feeling I strive to pass along to others.

Myth 4: Perfection Equals Connection

Perfectionism can paralyze you. I once blanked out during a presentation, forgot half my talking points, I remember clutching the index cards in my hands tightly, desperately trying to remember what I was supposed to say and stumbled through the ending. I was mortified. But afterward, someone said, "You were so real—it made you more relatable." That was my lightbulb moment.

Brené Brown's work shows that vulnerability builds stronger connections than perfection ever will (Brown, 2012). Chasing flawlessness blocks authenticity. Show up as you are—mistakes and all—and people will connect with your courage, not your script.

REMEMBER:

So many things can cause us to not believe in ourselves, such as negative experiences we've had in the past or playing the "what if" game but don't let the past prevent you from having a better future. Flip the "what if" question. Instead of asking: "*What if it all goes wrong?*", start asking

> "*What if it works out better than I imagined?*"

This small but positive shift in your mindset builds optimism and resilience.

Understanding Your Communication Style

What's Your Style?

Your communication style is like your social fingerprint. Maybe you're the chill observer who listens more than you talk. Or maybe you're bold and expressive, wearing your emotions on your sleeve. Neither is better—what matters is knowing your default.

Understanding your style makes a huge difference. Tools like DISC or the Myers-Briggs personality assessment can help. One of my own lightbulb moments came when I learned my directness could sometimes sound harsh. With that insight, I practiced softening my tone without diluting my message. Self-awareness is your superpower.

Recognizing your default communication patterns helps you

improve interactions significantly. Every person communicates uniquely. By identifying your style, you learn exactly where to improve and what strengths to leverage.

Reflect and Grow

Reflection is where real growth happens. After social situations, take a beat. What felt smooth? What felt awkward? What did you wish you'd said differently? Then ask a close friend for feedback—they might notice habits you miss.

Once, a friend told me, "You get so focused on being clear that you sometimes come across intense." It stung. But it helped. Now, I pause to check my delivery before jumping in. Honest feedback—paired with self-reflection—fast-tracks your evolution (Foster, 2014).

Adaptability is Your Superpower

Adaptability is a game-changer. When you adjust your communication style depending on who you're talking to, you become significantly more effective. Think of great communicators—Zendaya, Trevor Noah, even Billie Eilish. They shift effortlessly between interviews, performances, and real-talk convos with fans. That's adaptability. Being able to adjust your tone, language, and delivery based on your audience doesn't make you fake—it makes you effective.

Versatile communicators effortlessly shift their approach depending on context. Developing adaptability means strategically adjusting your communication to match different social, cultural, or professional environments, enhancing effectiveness and authenticity simultaneously.

Play to Your Strengths

We often overlook our own strengths because they come so naturally. Maybe you're funny. Empathetic. A great storyteller. Use those traits intentionally. If humor is your jam, use it to connect or diffuse tension. If you're a calm listener, anchor someone else's storm. Your strengths don't need fixing—they need featuring.

We often overlook our natural strengths because they feel effortless. Maybe you're funny, empathetic, or incredibly good at listening. Use these gifts intentionally in your conversations. If humor comes naturally, use it to diffuse tension. Leveraging your strengths authentically amplifies your communication skills (Buckingham & Clifton, 2001).

The Neuroscience of Connection

Ever noticed how smiles can feel contagious or how watching someone cry can tug at your heart? That's your brain's mirror neurons at work. Our brains are biologically wired for social interaction. Mirror neurons, activated when observing others, these amazing cells help us empathize by mirroring emotions we see in others (Iacoboni, 2009).

Our brains literally connect through emotions, laying the groundwork for empathy and deep connections. Understanding this biological foundation helps you consciously foster stronger emotional bonds in conversations.

Stress Less, Connect More

Stress can hijack your ability to communicate clearly. It negatively impacts cognitive functions vital for communication, such as focus and clarity. We've all experienced that moment when nerves turn our minds blank. Under pressure, your brain prioritizes threat management over conversational fluency.

Simple techniques like deep breathing or mindfulness can calm your brain, helping you stay focused and articulate. These regular relaxation techniques can significantly improve your communicative abilities (Kabat-Zinn, 2013). Managing stress isn't just good for your health—it's essential for clear communication.

Your Brain Can Change

Here's a fantastic thing about our brains: they're adaptable! Neuroplasticity means your brain's remarkable ability to rewire itself through experience, proves that communication skills can continuously improve at any age. We can continuously improve our communication skills through practice (Doidge, 2007). Every conversation you have, every skill you practice, strengthens new neural pathways, making effective communication second nature.

The Silent Power of Nonverbal Cues

Nonverbal signals—body language, facial expressions, and tone—significantly impact how your messages are received. Albert Mehrabian's research highlights the powerful role nonverbal cues play in emotional communication (Mehrabian, 1971). Aligning verbal and nonverbal communication enhances clarity and authenticity.

Setting Realistic Communication Goals

Effective goals can transform your communication. Using the SMART framework—Specific, Measurable, Achievable, Relevant, and Time-bound—helps you set clear objectives that push you forward without overwhelming you (Doran, 1981).

Example of a SMART Goal:

"I will practice speaking publicly by giving short 3-5 minute presentations in my class or local youth group at least three times each month for the next two months, aiming to steadily increase audience size and speaking time."

We've already established that the goal is to *Improve Public Speaking Skills*. Now, let's take a look at in action using the SMART framework:

- **Specific:** *"I will improve my ability to speak confidently in front of groups."*

- **Measurable:** *"I will speak at least three times per month in front of a small group or class."*

- **Achievable:** *"I will begin with familiar settings, such as study groups or close friends, and gradually move toward larger, less familiar audiences."*

- **Relevant:** *"Improving public speaking will boost my confidence for class presentations, interviews, and future career opportunities."*

- **Time-bound:** *"I will evaluate my progress and adjust my goals every two months."*

Scan or Clock to Download the **SMART Goal Planner.** Define clear objectives to improve specific communication skills.

SMART GOALS, SMART OUTCOMES!

Read the **Financial SMART Goals for Young Adults** article <https://roshelinarush.com/financial-smart-goals-for-young-adults/>

Tailor Your Goals

Make your goals personal. If speaking publicly terrifies you, start small. Practice in front of friends or record yourself speaking. Adjust your goals as you grow. Personalized goals feel achievable and meaningful.

Track and Celebrate

Track your progress with journaling and peer feedback, adjusting your goals as you improve. Don't forget to celebrate your milestones, even small ones. Celebrating keeps your motivation high and reminds you how far you've come.

Communication mastery is within your reach. It starts with challenging outdated myths, embracing your unique style, and committing to consistent growth. Trust the process—every conversation is a step forward, making you more skilled, authentic, and impactful.

By understanding your unique style, addressing hidden anxieties, and practicing targeted strategies, you're now ready to build lasting communication habits that empower and connect you with others authentically.

Chapter 1: Key Takeaways

- **Communication is a learned skill, not a fixed trait**—charisma and confidence grow through intentional practice, not perfection.

- **Active listening is powerful and engaging**, involving attention to body language, tone, and emotion—not just words.

- **Self-awareness and adaptability are communication superpowers**; knowing your style and adjusting it based on context builds connection.

- **Your brain is wired to connect—and can improve with use**; neuroplasticity means every conversation helps strengthen your communication habits.

- **Setting SMART goals accelerates your growth**, and tracking your progress (and celebrating wins) keeps your momentum going.

BECOMING A CONFIDENT COMMUNICATOR.

Chapter 1: Practical Action Points

1. Scan or Click to Download the **Communication Blueprint Worksheet.**

2. **Set SMART Goals:** Define clear objectives to improve specific communication skills.

3. **Seek Feedback and Reflect Regularly:** Engage trusted individuals for honest insights into your communication style. After conversations, assess what went well and identify areas for improvement.

4. **Practice Mindfulness:** Incorporate stress-reduction techniques to enhance communication clarity.

5. Read the **New Years Goal Setting For Student** article <https://roshelinarush.com/new-years-goal-setting-for-students/>

Chapter 2

Confidence in Conversation - From Awkward to Authentic

"Our deepest fear is not that we are inadequate. Our deepest fear is that we are powerful beyond measure... Who are you not to be?"

- Marianne Williamson

I magine standing at the entrance of a bustling networking event. Your heart races, palms grow clammy, and a voice inside whispers, *"Maybe I should just leave."* Sound familiar? You're not alone. Many of us have faced such moments of self-doubt. But here's the truth: confidence isn't the absence of fear; it's the courage to move forward despite it. With the right tools, you can navigate both in-person and digital social landscapes with assurance.

In this chapter, we'll explore practical strategies such as visualization techniques, positive affirmations, reframing rejection, and authentic self-expression—that can elevate your social confidence in today's interconnected world.

Picture this: you're at a party, and you see a group of people laughing and chatting effortlessly. They seem to be having the time of their lives. But you? You're standing on the sidelines, wishing you could join in. It feels like there's a barrier between you and them. You dream of being part of that group, but something holds you back. It's not that you don't want to connect. It's just hard to know where to start.

Visualization Techniques for Social Success

Real-Life Spotlight : When Mia, a university student with extreme social anxiety, was preparing for her first networking event, she didn't rehearse out loud—she visualized it. She pictured herself walking in, smiling, and asking a friendly question. It wasn't perfect, but she made three new connections that night. What helped her most? She had already "lived it" in her mind.

Just like athletes use mental rehearsal to perform under pressure, visualization can train your brain to behave with confidence—even before the moment arrives

Visualization: Your Mental Rehearsal

Visualization is a powerful tool that athletes have used for years. It's like a secret weapon they use before games to see themselves scoring a goal or winning a race. In sports psychology, this technique is called mental rehearsal. It involves practicing a task in your mind without physical movement. Research shows that visualization strengthens the brain's neural connections, making actual performance more effective. The good news is that you can use this same tool to boost your social skills. By imagining successful interactions, you prepare your mind to handle real-life situations with confidence.

Crafting Vivid Mental Imagery

tart by creating a vivid picture in your mind. Imagine walking into a room full of people. See yourself smiling, shaking hands, and starting conversations with ease. Picture the setting in detail. What does the room look like? What sounds do you hear? Engage all your senses. Smell the coffee brewing, feel the warmth of the room, and hear the buzz of chatter. This detailed mental imagery helps make the scenario feel real. It's like creating a mini-movie in your mind where you're the star. The more senses you involve, the more effective your visualization will be.

Before heading to a social event, spend a few minutes visualizing the interaction. Picture yourself at a networking event. Imagine approaching someone, introducing yourself, and talking about topics that interest you both. Visualize the conversation flowing smoothly. You can use a simple script in your mind.

For example, start with,

> "Hi, I'm [Your Name]. It's great to meet you. What brings you here today?"

Visualization in Digital Interactions

In today's digital age, social interactions often occur online. Before a video call or virtual meeting, visualize yourself speaking clearly, maintaining eye contact with the camera, and engaging participants effectively. This practice can reduce anxiety and enhance your virtual presence.

Practical Exercise

- Find a quiet space and close your eyes.

- Take deep breaths to center yourself.

- Visualize entering a social setting (physical or virtual) with confidence.

- Imagine initiating conversations and responding with ease.

Regular practice of this exercise can build neural pathways associated with confident social behavior.

Timing and frequency are key to effective visualization. Try to incorporate this practice into your daily routine. Spend about five to ten minutes each day visualizing different scenarios. The best time to do this is when you're relaxed, like before bed or after waking up. Consistent practice helps reinforce positive mental patterns. Over time, you'll notice a change in how you approach social situations. You'll feel more at ease and ready to engage with others.

The science behind visualization is fascinating. Studies show that the brain's activity during mental rehearsal is similar to physical practice. This means that even though you're not physically interacting, your brain is still working on building those connections. Visualization reduces anxiety, enhances confidence, and boosts performance. It's not just about seeing yourself succeed. It's about feeling that success and carrying that confidence into real interactions.

Positive Affirmations to Combat Anxiety

Real-Life Snapshot: Nadia used to dread speaking in Zoom meetings. She wrote a sticky note: *"I speak clearly and calmly."* Every morning, she read it while brushing her teeth. It sounded cheesy at first, but weeks later, her manager complimented her confidence. Repeating that one phrase helped her rewire her internal script—and it can help you, too.

Imagine you're about to speak in front of a crowd. The fear starts creeping in, and your heart races. It's that familiar feeling of anxiety. But what if you had a tool to quiet those nerves? This is where affirmations come in. They're positive statements that you say to yourself that reinforce your self-worth and capabilities. They help shift your mind from doubt to confidence.

Crafting Personalized Affirmations

Creating these affirmations is like building a personal mantra. It's something that speaks to you and your fears. For instance, if public speaking scares you, try an affirmation like,

> **"I am calm and confident when I speak."**

or

> **"I communicate my ideas clearly and confidently."**

The key is to make these affirmations personal. They should address what's holding you back.

Integrating Affirmations into Daily Life

Integrating affirmations into your daily life can be a game-changer. The idea is to make them a habit. Just like brushing your teeth. You can say them aloud when you wake up or before bed. Or maybe you prefer writing them down. It's all about finding what works for you. Technology can lend a hand here. Use apps or set reminders on your phone. Let them nudge you to repeat your affirmations throughout the day. The more you say them, the more they become a part of you.

Language is powerful. The words you choose shape how you see yourself. That's why affirmations should be in the present tense. They should feel real and immediate. Say, *"I am confident,"* instead of, *"I will be confident."* The present tense helps your brain believe it now. This is a technique rooted in cognitive behavioral therapy (CBT). CBT shows that changing your language can change your thoughts. It's about framing your self-talk in a way that boosts you up.

To know if affirmations are working, you need to check in with yourself. One way is through journaling. After using affirmations for a while, jot down how you feel. Are you less anxious? Do you approach social settings differently? Keeping track of changes helps you see patterns. It's like a personal experiment. You might find that some affirmations work better than others. If one doesn't feel right, tweak it. Make it yours. The goal is to find what truly resonates with you.

Incorporating affirmations into your routine can feel like having a small cheerleader in your corner. They remind you of your strengths and help you face challenges with a new mindset. It's not about pretending everything is perfect. It's about recognizing your potential and focusing on that. As you start this practice, remember it's about progress, not perfection. The more you engage with affirmations, the more natural they become. Eventually, they can become second nature, helping you tackle anxiety with a calm and confident mind.

> **Practical Tip:**
> Create a ***Confidence Mirror*** by sticking positive words and quotes on your mirror. Put photos of yourself and state some of your favorite features about yourself and personality on the mirror. This is a easy way to incorporate positive affirmations into your daily life.

Reframing Rejection as Opportunity

Real-Life Reset: When Jordan applied for a competitive internship and didn't get it, he felt crushed. But after journaling his thoughts, he realized the rejection wasn't about him—it was about timing and fit. That clarity gave him the courage to reapply to a better-fitting program, which he eventually got.

Understanding the Nature of Rejection

Rejection is an inevitable part of social interactions. It doesn't define your worth—it often reflects a mismatch in timing, needs, or circumstances. By changing how you view rejection, you unlock growth and resilience.

Strategies for Cognitive Reframing

- Shift Perspective: Instead of asking "What did I do wrong?", ask "What can I learn from this?"

- Normalize Rejection: Everyone experiences it. It's not a stop sign—it's a signal to redirect.

- Celebrate the Effort: The courage to show up matters more than the outcome. A "no" means you tried—and that counts.

Building Resilience Through Reflection

Start a simple journal practice:

- Record rejections (big or small).

- Note how they made you feel.

- Identify one insight gained.

Over time, you'll see patterns of growth—and your ability to handle rejection will strengthen naturally.

The Ladder of Inference
One tool that can help you reframe rejection is the **Ladder of Inference**—a framework used in psychology and leadership training. When someone rejects you, your brain quickly climbs this "ladder":

- **You observe their behavior (e.g., They didn't reply to your message).**

- **You assign meaning (e.g., "They're ignoring me.")**

- **You make assumptions (e.g., "They don't like me.")**

- **You form beliefs (e.g., "I'm not good at making friends.")**

To reframe, pause at each step:

- **What *actually* happened?**

- **What *else* could it mean?**

- **What assumption am I making?**

This helps you slow down reactive thinking and gain perspective.

The Power of Authentic Self-Expression

Real-Life Reveal: Leila used to hide her love for fantasy novels because she thought it made her "uncool" at networking events. The day she brought it up during a conversation, someone said, "No way, me too!"—and a real connection formed.

Authenticity is magnetic. When you show up as yourself, you attract relationships that are aligned with your values—not a performance.

Embracing Authenticity in Communication

Overcoming Barriers to Authenticity

- Self-Awareness: Reflect on what lights you up. What parts of yourself do you keep hidden in public?

- Courage: Vulnerability can feel risky, but it creates space for real connection.

- Boundaries: Being authentic doesn't mean oversharing. Know what's appropriate for the space you're in.

Johari Window Model

The Johari Window is a psychological tool that explores self-awareness and authenticity in relationships. It has four "windows":

- **1 | Open:** Things known to you and others (e.g., hobbies you talk about).

- **2 | Hidden:** Things you know but don't share (e.g., fears, insecurities).

- **3 | Blind:** What others see that you don't (e.g., your tone or energy).

- **4 | Unknown:** Untapped potential or patterns not yet revealed.

Action Step:
Share something from your "Hidden" quadrant with someone you trust. Notice how it deepens the connection.

Authenticity in Digital Interactions

Online, it's easy to curate a perfect version of yourself. But realness matters here, too. Instead of posting only highlight reels like you see other people doing on Instagram, occasionally share a behind-the-scenes moment or a personal insight. It builds trust.

Try This:

- Pick one area where you feel you're "editing" yourself too much (online or in-person).

- Share something genuine. It can be as small as a real opinion or a less-than-perfect story.

- Reflect: Did it feel scary? Liberating? What kind of response did you get?

Managing Digital Overwhelm

Real-Life Reboot: After realizing she spent four hours daily on social media, Priya started limiting her screen time to 30 minutes in the morning and 30 minutes at night. Within a week, her stress dipped—and she finally finished reading a book she'd started months ago.

Recognizing Digital Overload

Digital overload is real. Constant pings, notifications, and scrolling can flood your brain, drain your energy, and heighten anxiety in social settings.

Recognizing the Signs:

- Feeling irritable or "foggy" after using your phone

- Difficulty focusing in conversations

- Needing to check your device every few minutes

Strategies to Regain Control

- Set Boundaries: Schedule tech-free windows (e.g., during meals or before bed).

- Curate Your Feed: Unfollow accounts that leave you feeling inadequate, overwhelmed, or drained.

- **Designate Tech-Free Zones:** Your bed, bathroom, and dining table are great places to start.

Mindful Engagement Tip:

Before opening an app or replying to a message, pause. Ask: ***"Why am I opening this? What do I want to get from it?"*** Intentional usage rewires your digital habits. Engage with digital content intentionally to avoid mindless consumption.

Framework: The Digital Well-being Pyramid
Think of your digital habits like a food pyramid:

- **Base layer (Foundation):** Sleep, in-person connection, movement

- **Middle layer:** Mindful screen use for learning, work, and inspiration

- **Top layer (Limit):** Passive scrolling, notifications, doomscrolling

Use this to assess how much "digital nutrition" you're getting. Are you over-consuming the top layer and underfeeding your base?

By integrating these strategies into your daily life, you'll cultivate a robust sense of confidence that transcends social settings, empowering you to navigate both the physical and digital worlds with authenticity and ease.

Tailoring Your Confidence Style: For Introverts and Extroverts

There's no one-size-fits-all when it comes to confidence. Some people gain energy from social interaction; others recharge through solitude. Your social confidence doesn't need to mimic anyone else's—it should feel true to *you*.

If You're More Introverted

- **Start Small, Go Deep:** Focus on meaningful 1:1 conversations rather than trying to "work the room."

- **Pre-plan Touchpoints:** Have a few questions or openers ready before events. This keeps your mind calm and focused.

- **Leverage Quiet Strengths:** Your listening skills and thoughtfulness are communication superpowers. Use them to create deeper bonds.

- **Choose Energizing Spaces:** Attend settings that feel aligned—like workshops, community events, or small group hangouts.

Quiet Leader Spotlight:
Marcus, a soft-spoken data analyst, dreaded work socials. But he offered to lead small breakout groups instead of large

presentations. Now, colleagues turn to him for his insight—and his presence is trusted, not loud.

If You're More Extroverted

- **Use Energy to Connect:** Channel your enthusiasm into helping others feel welcomed. Initiate, but make space.

- **Practice Mindful Listening:** Be aware of when you're dominating the conversation. Pause, reflect, and invite others in.

- **Balance Social Bursts:** After highly social days, recharge with solo activities to avoid burnout.

- **Go Beyond Surface:** You're great at making first impressions—now practice guiding conversations deeper.

Growth Tip: Whether introvert or extrovert, confidence grows fastest when you respect your energy and stretch it—not force it.

Chapter 2: Key Takeaway

- **Confidence is built, not born**—techniques like visualization and positive affirmations can rewire your brain to handle social settings with courage and calm.

- **Rejection is redirection**—by reframing rejection through journaling and reflection, you gain resilience and clarity for better future outcomes.

- **Authenticity creates real connection**—owning your true interests and values builds stronger, more meaningful relationships in both in-person and digital spaces.

- **Mindful digital use boosts confidence**—setting healthy tech boundaries improves focus, energy, and your ability to show up with presence.

- **Introvert or extrovert, confidence is personal**—tailor your growth strategies to align with your natural energy, and stretch without forcing.

Chapter 2: Practical Action Points

- **Daily Visualization:** Dedicate five minutes each day to visualize successful social interactions, both in-person and online.

- **Affirmation Practice:** Develop three personal affirmations and recite them during your morning routine.

- **Rejection Journal:** After experiencing rejection, write down the event, your feelings, and insights gained.

- **Authenticity Challenge:** Share something genuine about yourself in a conversation or on social media this week.

- **Digital Detox:** Implement a "no screens" rule for the first hour after waking and the hour before bedtime.

Small Talk, Big Impact - Turning Casual Chats into Connections

"Ultimately, the bond of all companionship, whether in marriage or friendship, is conversation."

- Oscar Wilde

Have you ever been in a situation where the silence felt painfully loud, and you desperately wished you knew exactly what to say? Trust me, we've all been there—staring at the floor, fiddling with our phones, or pretending to check messages that don't exist. You're not alone. I've had my fair share of awkward silences and uncomfortable conversations too.

Here's the thing: small talk doesn't have to be awkward or pointless. In fact, mastering small talk is your gateway to meaningful conversations and lasting connections, especially in our digital-driven world. I've discovered that small talk isn't just empty chatter—it's a powerful entryway to meaningful dialogue and deeper relationships, both offline and online.

In this chapter, you'll discover practical strategies for crafting engaging icebreakers, transitioning smoothly from casual chats to deeper discussions, using storytelling to captivate, and even handling silences like a pro, all tailored specifically for young adults navigating today's digital landscape.

Why Small Talk is a Big Deal

Let's clear one thing up right away: Small talk matters—a lot. Think of it as conversational lubricant. It smooths interactions, eases anxiety, and fosters an initial connection. According to Alison Wood Brooks (2019), engaging in small talk reduces stress and primes your mind for deeper, more genuine exchanges.

Every lasting relationship or valuable connection usually begins with seemingly insignificant chatter about the weather, hobbies, or weekend plans. These conversations help establish rapport, trust, and comfort, making deeper topics accessible and appropriate.

Crafting the Perfect Icebreaker

Picture this: you're at a gathering, and the room buzzes with chatter. You spot someone you'd like to talk to, but your mind goes blank. You wonder how to start a conversation without sounding awkward. We've all been there. It's that moment of hesitation that makes social situations feel daunting. But what if I told you that a simple icebreaker could change everything?

Icebreakers are like the keys to a locked door. They open up conversations, making it easier to connect with others. They're not just for breaking the ice or getting past that initial awkwardness. They set the tone for everything that follows. A well-placed icebreaker can turn a stiff, transactional interaction into a genuine connection.

Why Icebreakers Matter

When you meet someone new, you both form impressions within 7 seconds. That's not just a saying—it's backed by research in social psychology (Berkowitz, 2012). Remember, first impressions matter. This is where the magic of icebreakers comes in. Icebreakers help ease tension and create a welcoming atmosphere. They work by reducing anxiety and making people feel comfortable.

Think of it like warming up before a workout. It gets the social muscles moving and makes everything that follows flow better. A great icebreaker transforms an awkward intro into a friendly exchange, paving the way for more engaging and meaningful conversations.

There's no one-size-fits-all when it comes to icebreakers. Your approach should match the setting and the tone of the event. The most effective icebreakers fit the context:

- If you're at a professional networking mixer, keep things respectful and focused. Try:

> **"What do you enjoy most about your work?"** or **"What brought you to this event today?"**

- In a more casual setting, you can afford to be playful and relaxed. At a party, asking:

> **"What's the weirdest snack you've tried?"** or **"Which artist do you secretly listen to on repeat?"**

This makes people laugh and lowers their guard. You can even try an oldie but a goodie:

> **"Seen any great shows or movies lately?"**

Cultural awareness also plays a big role. What's charming or clever in one culture may be misunderstood or off-putting in another. Adjusting your icebreakers based on the audience shows emotional intelligence and respect. Always consider your audience's background and interests.

Humor and Curiosity: The Ultimate Duo

Humor and curiosity are two of your most powerful communication tools. Humor lightens the mood and makes you memorable. Curiosity invites people to share and connect.

A well-timed joke like:

> *"So, are you here for the free snacks or the actual event?"*

can disarm social tension. Research from Stanford University shows that humor not only increases likeability but also enhances perceived competence and status in social interactions (Lammers & Gast, 2017).

Curiosity, on the other hand, deepens engagement. Questions like:

> *"What's something fun you've done recently?"* or *"If you had a free weekend with no responsibilities, how would you spend it?"*

These show that you're genuinely interested in the other person, not just making small talk for the sake of it. As Bruess (2022) noted in her article titles *"Why Curiosity in Conversations Is Key to a Healthy Relationship"*, curiosity in conversation enhances empathy and leads to healthier, more enjoyable interactions.

Nailing Your Delivery

Delivery is everything. Practice your icebreakers in low-pressure settings with friends or family first. A great icebreaker can fall flat if the delivery is off. You don't need to be overly rehearsed, but some preparation goes a long way. Pay attention to your tone—be warm, upbeat, and genuine. Your body language also matters: a friendly smile, maintain good eye contact, and use open gestures significantly enhance your approach.

Timing is everything. You don't want to blurt out your icebreaker while someone's mid-conversation or clearly preoccupied. Look for a natural pause or moment of eye contact to engage. The more you practice, the more intuitive your timing will become.

Icebreaker Practice Exercise

Take a moment to brainstorm three different social scenarios you might find yourself in—a work event, a friend's party, and a virtual meetup. For each one, write down two or three relevant icebreakers. Say them out loud. Notice how they feel. Are they natural to you? Would they make you smile if someone asked you?

You can even role-play with a friend or test them in real conversations. Over time, you'll build a personal collection of go-to openers that help you start conversations with ease.

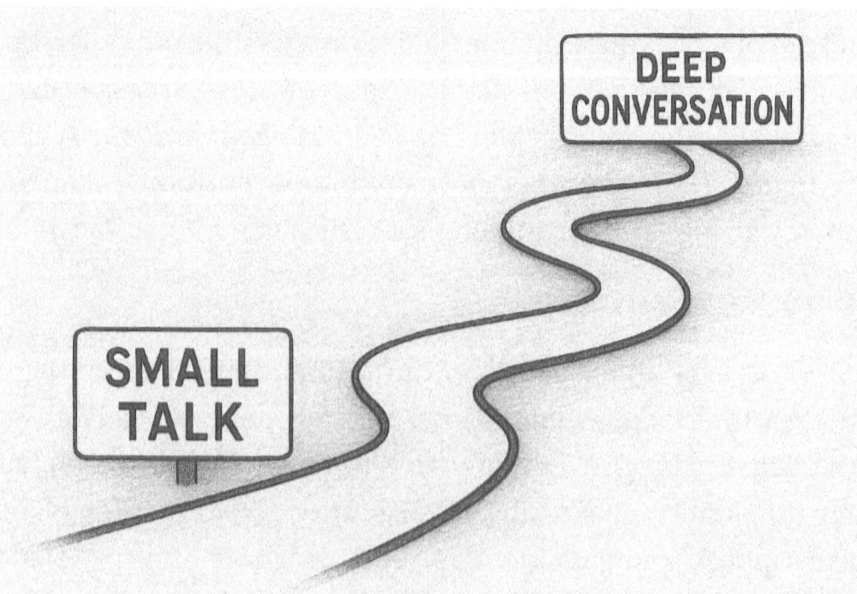

Transitioning from Small Talk to Deep Conversations

We've all been stuck in small talk loops—the weather, weekend plans, *"What do you do?"*—and wished we could get to the good stuff. So how do you move past surface-level chatter into meaningful conversation?

Spotting Opportunities to Go Deeper

Look for cues: Is the other person leaning in? Are they nodding, maintaining eye contact, or asking follow-up questions? These are green lights for going deeper.

Once you spot those signs, use bridge phrases like:

> **"That reminds me..."** or **"I'd love to hear more about..."**

to guide the conversation. If they mention a concert, ask about their music taste. If they talk about a vacation, ask what made it special. The key is curiosity and listening for openings. Nonverbal signals often reveal more than words alone.

Smooth Transitions

Use transitional phrases to move naturally into more meaningful topics:

- "You mentioned you enjoy traveling—what's been your most memorable trip?"

- "It sounds like you're really passionate about this. Can you tell me more?"

Finding Common Ground and Building on Common Interests

Finding shared ground is like striking conversational gold. Common ground creates instant rapport and keeps conversations flowing naturally. If you both love the same podcast or Netflix series, talk about what drew you to it. If you've both traveled somewhere, share what you loved or struggled with. If you both enjoy digital photography, explore each other's favorite editing apps or social media platforms.

The goal isn't just to find a topic—it's to explore it together. Quickly identify shared interests, hobbies, or experiences. Ask follow-up questions, share your perspective, and let the conversation evolve naturally. The best talks feel like a game of catch, not an interview.

Getting Real: Openness and Vulnerability

One of the most powerful ways to take conversations deeper is by being real. You don't have to overshare, but offering a personal story or challenge shows that you trust the other person. This often invites them to open up too.

You might say,

> *"Honestly, I've been nervous about events like this, but I'm trying to push myself out of my comfort zone."*

That one line says a lot: you're human, honest, and open to

growth. Vulnerability builds trust. And trust builds relationships. Create a safe space by responding without judgment and showing genuine interest in what the other person has to say or share with you.

Maintaining Interest with Relatable Stories

The Art of Storytelling in Conversation

Stories bring conversations to life and as Humans we are wired to love stories. They're how we make sense of the world, connect with others, and make interactions memorable. A good story is more than just a timeline—it has emotion, texture, and a message.

Crafting Your Story

Think about moments in your life that taught you something, made you laugh, or changed your perspective. Practice telling them in a way that flows and feels true to you. Keep it tight—cut the fluff and focus on the heart of the story. For instance, rather than listing job duties, share an amusing anecdote about a challenge you overcame.

A compelling story has a clear structure: a beginning that sets the scene, a middle that shares the experience, and an end that delivers a clear point.

Aligning Stories with Your Audience Interests

Adapt your stories to your audience. A funny story about a college mishap might kill at a party, but feel out of place in a formal setting. Learn to read the room.

Tailor stories to your listener's background and interests. If speaking to students, choose stories about your educational journey or early career experiences. Adapt based on the feedback you receive, keeping stories flexible and engaging.

Using Humor and Emotion in Stories Effectively

A story without emotion is just a report. But too much emotion without humor can feel heavy. The best storytellers find the sweet spot. They balance humor with sincerity which creates depth, captures attention and evoke empathy, making their stories memorable and resonant.

Emotional hooks—like overcoming setbacks or sharing meaningful lessons—draw people in, fostering deeper connections. A dash of humor makes you relatable. A touch of vulnerability makes you trustworthy. Together, they make you unforgettable.

Overcoming the Fear of Awkward Silences

Understanding the Dynamics of Silence

Silences happen naturally and aren't inherently negative. They often indicate thoughtful reflection or comfort. Instead of fearing silence, view it as a normal part of conversation dynamics.

Strategies for Navigating Awkward Silences Gracefully

Reframe silence as a natural pause for thought. When silence occurs, take a deep breath, maintain a relaxed posture, and gently reinitiate conversation with an open-ended question or observation about your surroundings.

Using Silence Strategically to Your Advantage

Silence can prompt others to share deeper thoughts. When

someone pauses, resist the urge to jump in immediately. Allowing space encourages reflection and more meaningful dialogue.

Building Comfort with Silence

Let's talk about the elephant in the room: awkward silence. You say something, they pause. You freeze. Panic sets in. Sound familiar?

Silence can feel uncomfortable, especially in digital spaces where delays and glitches are common. But silence doesn't have to mean something's wrong. It often just means someone is thinking—or maybe they're introverted and taking a moment.

Instead of fearing silence, use it. Pause after making a point. Let your words land. Give people space to gather their thoughts. You'll be surprised how often those quiet moments lead to the most thoughtful responses.

According to *The Financial Times* (2023), silence is a powerful conversational tool that promotes deeper reflection and understanding. The best communicators often use pauses to invite dialogue and highlight the importance of their message.

When you're faced with an awkward silence, try gently restarting the conversation with something simple like,

> **"That got me thinking—have you ever...?"** or **"What's your take on that?"**

You're not only moving things forward—you're inviting them back in.

Mindfulness practices help you manage anxiety around silence.

Focus on breathing deeply, grounding yourself in the present moment, and accepting silence as a normal, valuable aspect of conversation.

By integrating these techniques into your social toolkit, you'll effortlessly navigate conversations from initial introductions to meaningful dialogues—making lasting connections both offline and in the digital realm.

Mastering small talk isn't about being smooth or saying all the right things. It's about being present, curious, and willing to connect. Start with a strong icebreaker, follow the flow of the conversation, and let your authenticity guide you.

Whether it's a quick chat at a party or a virtual coffee catch-up, these skills will help you build confidence and turn everyday interactions into opportunities for real connection.

Chapter 3: Key Takeaways

- **Small talk is a powerful gateway** to deeper connection – it reduces anxiety, builds rapport, and sets the tone for meaningful conversation.

- **Effective icebreakers are context-sensitive and personal** – use humor and curiosity to start conversations, and tailor your approach to the social setting and cultural background.

- **Deep conversations evolve naturally from attentive listening** – look for cues, ask bridge questions, and find common ground to move beyond surface-level chatter.

- **Relatable stories spark interest and trust** – keep them concise, emotionally engaging, and appropriate for your audience and context.

- **Silence isn't awkward—it's strategic** – embracing and using silence can lead to deeper reflection, thoughtful dialogue, and greater comfort in conversation.

<u>Chapter 3: Practical Action Points</u>

- **Prepare and practice:** Write down three context-specific icebreakers for professional, social, and digital settings. Practice them until they feel natural.

- **Practice silence:** Try Intentionally pausing in conversations this week when talking to others, becoming comfortable with brief silences and observing how positively they can impact your interactions.

- **Use transition phrases:** In your next conversation, consciously use a transition phrase to deepen the dialogue.

- **Craft relatable stories:** Develop two relatable stories you can share confidently, ensuring they are relevant to your typical conversational settings.

CHAPTER 4
Listening That Connects - The Hidden Power of Empathy

"Most people do not listen with the intent to understand; they listen with the intent to reply."

- Stephen R. Covey

Picture this: you're at a lively family dinner. Everyone's sharing stories, laughter fills the room, but your mind is miles away. You're nodding, maybe even smiling, yet you're not really there.

We've all been in moments like this, where we hear words but miss the meaning. This is where active listening comes into play. It's not just about hearing sounds. It's about truly engaging and understanding the speaker.

You've probably heard it a million times: "Just listen." But let's be honest—most of us think we're better listeners than we actually are. The truth is, hearing and truly listening are not the same thing. Hearing is passive. Listening is active, intentional, and deeply rooted in presence. And in the digital age—where attention spans are short and distractions are constant—mastering the art of active listening is more essential than ever.

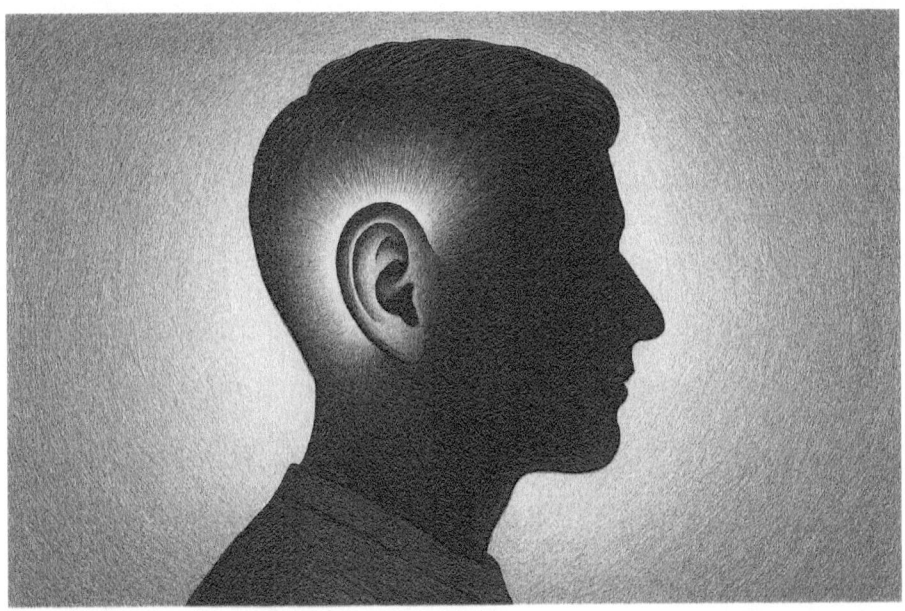

What is Active Listening (and Why It Matters)

Active listening is more than nodding your head while someone else is talking. It means giving your full, undivided attention. It's about being present, mentally and emotionally, and demonstrating that you genuinely care about what the other person is saying. According to research from Wright State University, active listening improves understanding, reduces conflict, and builds stronger relationships (Brownell, 2012).

Active listening is more than just a skill. It's a bridge to deeper connections and clearer communication. When you actively listen, you focus on the speaker, putting aside your own thoughts and distractions. This transforms simple exchanges into meaningful conversations.

To be an active listener, you must:

- **Avoid distractions.** Put your phone down. Close extra browser tabs.

- **Make eye contact.** This shows that you're engaged and present.

- **Use verbal cues.** Phrases like "I see," "Go on," or "Tell me more" signal that you're tuned in.

- **Paraphrase or summarize.** Saying something like, "So what you're saying is..." helps confirm understanding.

These small behaviors make a huge difference. They validate the speaker and create a space where authentic conversation can unfold.

Common Listening Barriers (and How to Overcome Them)

Let's face it—active listening is hard. Your mind wanders. You're thinking about your to-do list or what you're going to say next. That's normal. But being aware of these internal distractions is the first step to managing them.

Here are some common barriers:

- **Internal distractions.** Combat them by taking a deep breath before conversations and gently re-focusing when your mind drifts.

- **Judging too quickly.** Try to listen without forming immediate opinions or jumping to conclusions.

- **Interrupting.** Resist the urge to finish someone's sentence. Let them speak fully.

Practice mindfulness techniques to stay grounded. If the conversation is long, take mental notes and circle back to important points. This shows you care and keeps the discussion on track.

Evaluate Your Listening Skills

Want to know how good you really are at listening? Reflect on a recent conversation:

- Did you remember key details the other person shared?

- Did you wait until they finished before responding?

- Did you ask questions to clarify?

Journaling your reflections after conversations can help you spot patterns and improve over time.

The Power of Empathy in Communication

Empathy is the ability to understand and share the feelings of another person. In communication, empathy means stepping into someone else's shoes—not just hearing their words, but feeling their emotions.

Studies from the University of California, Berkeley show that empathy fosters trust and emotional bonding, which are essential for deeper and more meaningful conversations (Decety & Jackson, 2006). In conflict resolution, empathy helps de-escalate tension and promotes collaborative problem-solving.

To practice empathy:

- Ask open-ended questions: "How did that make you feel?"

- Acknowledge their emotions: "That sounds really frustrating."

- Avoid jumping into problem-solving mode. Sometimes, people just want to be heard.

Empathy Across Cultures and Contexts

Empathy isn't one-size-fits-all. Cultural background, personal values, and lived experiences all shape how people express and interpret emotions. That's why cross-cultural empathy is so important, especially in today's global and digital world.

If you're talking with someone from a different cultural background:

- Be aware of different communication norms (e.g., some cultures value directness, others prefer subtlety).

- Practice humility. Assume there's more you don't know.

- Ask questions rather than making assumptions.

Emotional Intelligence and Empathy

Empathy is a key component of emotional intelligence (EQ), which also includes self-awareness, emotional regulation, and social skills. When your EQ is strong, you can navigate complex conversations with grace.

To boost your emotional intelligence:

- Pay attention to your own feelings during conversations.

- Learn to manage emotional triggers.

- Practice responding instead of reacting.

According to Goleman (1995), emotionally intelligent individuals are more successful in both personal and professional relationships because they understand how emotions affect communication.

Reading Between the Lines: Understanding Subtext

Sometimes, it's not what's said—it's what's left unsaid that matters most. Subtext refers to the hidden meaning behind the words. It shows up in tone, body language, and choice of words. Learning to pick up on subtext helps you understand the full emotional context of a conversation.

Watch for:
- **Tone of voice:** Sarcasm, hesitation, excitement.

- **Body language:** Crossed arms, shifting posture, lack of eye contact.

- **Facial expressions:** A smile that doesn't reach the eyes.

If you suspect a hidden message, ask gentle clarifying questions like,

> "You said you're fine—do you really feel that way?"

or

> "I noticed you paused—do you want to say more about that?"

Avoid assuming the worst. Verify with curiosity, not judgment.

Finding the Balance: Listening and Speaking

Great conversations have rhythm. If one person dominates, it can feel draining or performative. On the other hand, holding back too much can create distance. Striking the right balance means:

- Knowing when to contribute.

- Pausing to invite the other person in.

- Sharing your perspective while staying open to theirs.

Practice this:

- Use the 50/50 rule in conversations: aim to speak half the time and listen the other half.

- If you notice you're doing most of the talking, pause and ask, "What do you think?"

Learning to balance dialogue creates a collaborative and energizing communication experience.

Being a great communicator doesn't mean always having the right words—it means knowing how to truly listen, understand, and connect.

In this chapter, we've unpacked the vital role of active listening, the depth that empathy brings to conversations, and the power of reading between the lines. These aren't just communication tools—they're relationship-builders. They help you earn trust, defuse tension, and form deeper bonds in every area of life. In a world that's always talking, the people who know how to listen stand out. Be one of them.

As we continue this journey, remember that mastering communication isn't about being perfect. It's about being present. You don't have to say everything right—you just have to care enough to hear what others really mean.

Chapter 4: Key Takeaways

- **Active listening transforms conversations**—it requires full presence, eye contact, and verbal cues that show genuine engagement and care.

- **Common distractions can be overcome**—by practicing mindfulness and resisting the urge to interrupt or judge, you make space for deeper connection.

- **Empathy builds trust and understanding**—asking open-ended questions and acknowledging emotions fosters safe, meaningful dialogue.

- **Reading subtext adds depth**—tone, body language, and pauses often reveal more than words; verify gently, without assumptions.

- **Balanced dialogue is key**—aim for a conversational rhythm where both speaking and listening are equally valued, making space for true connection.

Chapter 4: Practical Action Points

- **Practice mindful listening:** In your next conversation, focus on the other person without distractions for at least five minutes.

- **Use the phrase "Tell me more"** to deepen engagement.

- **After a conversation, journal one thing you learned about the other person** and one area you could improve.

- **Watch a video or show with the sound off**—observe facial expressions and body language. Try to interpret what's being communicated.

- **Identify one situation this week to intentionally practice empathy**—and note how it shifts the conversation.

Text, DM, or Talk? - Mastering Communication in a Digital World

"The way we communicate with others and with ourselves ultimately determines the quality of our lives."

- Tony Robbins

We live in a world where communication is as likely to happen over a screen as it is face-to-face.

A message, emoji, or voice note can spark new relationships or misunderstandings.

Welcome to the digital age of communication, where tone, timing, and clarity are often lost in translation. Mastering the art of digital conversation isn't just a helpful skill anymore - it's a survival tool.

This chapter is your guide to navigating online conversations with confidence and clarity. We'll unpack how to start and sustain meaningful digital dialogues, use social media responsibly, understand emojis and punctuation cues, and manage digital overwhelm in a hyper-connected world.

Whether you're sliding into a DM, replying to a group chat, or sending a work email, these skills will help you stay clear, confident, and connected.

Crafting Compelling Digital Conversations

Understand the Dynamics of Digital Communication

Digital communication isn't just a replacement for face-to-face interaction—it's its own language. In real life, body language, eye contact, and vocal tone fill in the gaps between our words. Online? All of that disappears. This absence of nonverbal cues can make texts feel colder or more confusing than intended (Derks, Fischer, & Bos, 2008).

Timing plays a huge role, too. A delayed response can feel like a rejection. A fast reply might be seen as overly eager. There's a psychological layer to digital interactions that's easy to misinterpret. That's why digital conversations require more thoughtfulness and care.

Timing Depends on Context: Personal vs. Professional vs. Cultural

In today's digital-first environment, timing is not inherently "good" or "bad," but highly context-dependent. Interpretation varies by setting:

- **Professional Contexts**: In workplace communication

(e.g., email, Slack), quick responses can signal efficiency and reliability, especially during work hours. However, replying too fast to every message—even outside of working hours—can set unrealistic expectations for availability and affect work-life balance.

- **Personal Contexts**: Among close friends or romantic partners, quicker replies are often expected and can signal emotional closeness or investment. Delays may create anxiety if the relationship already has unresolved issues or insecurities.

- **Cultural and Generational Factors**: Some cultures place higher value on real-time communication (e.g., certain Asian and Middle Eastern contexts), while others (such as many Northern European cultures) may interpret a delay as a sign of respect for boundaries. Similarly, Gen Z may expect fast replies via DMs or texts, while older generations may be more comfortable with asynchronous communication.

You need to consider the nature of the relationship, the platform used, and cultural or professional norms before making assumptions based on response time.

Techniques for Engaging Online Dialogue

Want to be more engaging online?

Ask open-ended questions like,

"What was the best part of your week?" or *"What's your take on this?"*

These kinds of questions invite real responses instead of one-word answers. Respond promptly—but thoughtfully. A fast reply shows you're engaged, but taking a moment to think shows you care about the response.

Personalizing Digital Interactions

Here's a secret: people want to feel seen—even online. Use their name. Reference something they said earlier. Tailor your message to their tone or interests.

Research shows that personalization increases user satisfaction and makes communication more effective (Kalyanaraman & Sundar, 2006). For example, if someone ends their message with a laughing emoji, it's okay to respond playfully.

These personal touches transform your messages from robotic to human.

Balancing Professional and Personal Tones

Digital communication ranges from Slack messages to LinkedIn comments to casual Instagram DMs. Knowing your audience and adjusting your tone is essential. A good rule of thumb: when in doubt, be slightly more formal.

Use emojis sparingly in professional settings (a thumbs-up is generally safe). Keep it concise but warm—think,

"Hi Maya, thanks for getting back to me! I really appreciate it."

Etiquette for Social Media Interaction

Understanding Social Media Norms

Each platform has its own unspoken rules. LinkedIn? Professional. Instagram? More casual. TikTok? Quirky, creative, and fast-paced. Being aware of these nuances helps you blend in naturally and avoid accidental faux pas.

For example, what's acceptable on Instagram Stories may not fly in a professional context on LinkedIn.

- **Platform Evolution**: LinkedIn, once considered purely professional, has evolved. Personal storytelling, vulnerability, and even memes are now gaining traction—especially when tied to leadership or lessons. Instagram, on the other hand, may shift toward more curated or influencer-style content, depending on one's niche or audience.

- **Audience Matters**: A user might maintain a humorous and informal tone on Instagram with close friends but adopt a more polished, strategic persona on the same platform if building a brand or attracting professional opportunities. Similarly, someone might post a casual "day-in-the-life" update on LinkedIn if their audience is in the creative or tech industries where personal branding is valued.

- **Nuance in Humor and Authenticity**: You have to "read the room" before posting. For instance, sarcasm or humor that works on Twitter (now X) might fall flat on Facebook or LinkedIn, where tone is harder to interpret without shared context.

Crafting Thoughtful Social Media Posts

Be intentional with what you post. Ask yourself: Is this valuable, respectful, or inspiring? Use relevant hashtags to boost reach, tag people when it makes sense, and avoid oversharing. Research shows that personalization increases user satisfaction and makes communication more effective (Kalyanaraman & Sundar, 2006).

Frequency matters, too—posting too often can feel spammy; too little can make you invisible.

Responding to Comments and Messages

Whether someone's hyping you up or giving you criticism, always respond with respect. If someone leaves a thoughtful comment, acknowledge it. If they post something negative, don't jump into defense mode. Pause, breathe, and respond with curiosity or clarification.

> *"Thanks for sharing your thoughts—can you tell me more about what you meant?"*

diffuses tension and opens the door to conversation.

Privacy and Boundaries on Social Media

Just because you can share everything doesn't mean you should, this was a lesson I had to learn the hard way. Set clear boundaries. Adjust your privacy settings. Avoid posting sensitive personal details like your location in real-time or relationship conflicts.

Protect your mental space, too. It's okay to mute, unfollow, or block accounts that drain your energy.

Decoding Emojis and Textual Cues

The Role of Emojis in Digital Communication

Believe it or not, emojis are powerful emotional signals. A simple "Thanks " feels warmer than "Thanks." Emojis help replace tone and expression lost in text. But be mindful—different emojis mean different things to different people and cultures. What's flirty in one context might be friendly in another. Studies show that emojis enhance perceived emotionality and interpersonal warmth (Ganster, Eimler, & Krämer, 2012).

Interpreting Common Emojis and Symbols

Not all emojis are universal. The might mean "I'm joking" to one person and passive-aggressiveness to another. When in doubt, keep it simple and avoid overusing emojis in formal communication. In professional emails, skip the and stick to clear words.

Textual Cues Beyond Emojis

Tone can also be shaped by how you type. Ending a sentence with a period might feel cold ("Okay.") while no punctuation might feel casual ("Okay"). Using ellipses ("Sure...") can imply hesitation or sarcasm. Overusing exclamation marks might come across as trying too hard. Learn to read between the lines—and write with care.

Managing Digital Overwhelm

Identifying Signs of Digital Fatigue

If you've ever felt mentally drained after scrolling or replying to messages, you're not alone. Constant connectivity can lead to digital fatigue. Signs include brain fog, irritability, and a sense of being "always on." According to the American Psychological Association, the average screen time for young adults exceeds 7 hours a day, contributing to stress and disrupted sleep (APA, 2023).

Strategies for Digital Detox

You don't need to disappear offline—but setting boundaries is key. Try this:

- Set specific times to check messages and emails.

- Use Do Not Disturb mode during meals or focused work.

- Uninstall apps that aren't serving you.

- Try screen-free mornings or evenings.

These micro-breaks can massively improve your mental clarity and energy (Kushlev & Dunn, 2015).

Prioritizing Digital Interactions

You don't have to respond to everything immediately. Triage your messages:

- Urgent (respond within an hour)

- Important (respond within a day)

- Low-priority (batch these once or twice a week)

Use folders, filters, or tools like "snooze" and "schedule send" to manage your inbox efficiently.

Staying Focused in a Noisy Digital World

Digital multitasking feels productive—but it often reduces the quality of your communication. Try:

- Turning off non-essential notifications.

- Using website blockers for focus sessions.

- Practicing digital mindfulness: Before you respond to a message, pause. Take a breath. Then reply with clarity.

You don't need to keep up with everything. You just need to be intentional about what you engage with.

In the digital world, your words travel fast and far—often without the help of facial expressions or tone. This chapter equips you to show up online with presence, clarity, and intention. Because how you communicate digitally is just as important as how you do it in person. Maybe even more so because you're words can live online forever, even when you delete them, it's never truely gone.

Let's make every tap, type, and tweet count.

Social Media Tone Cheat Sheet

Platform	Audience	Typical Tone	Evolving Trends
LinkedIn	Professional	Formal to semi-formal	Personal storytelling on the rise
Instagram	Friends / Public	Casual, expressive	More curated or branded content
TikTok	Broad Gen Z base	Quirky, humorous	Educational/informal hybrids
Twitter/X	Mixed	Sarcastic, brief	Thought leadership & hot takes

Chapter 5: Key Takeaways

- **Digital conversations require extra intention** – without body language or tone, clarity, timing, and empathy become even more critical.

- **Personalization makes you stand out online** – use names, reference past messages, and match tone to create authentic digital connection.

- **Respect digital tone and platform norms** – adjust your communication style depending on whether you're on LinkedIn, Instagram, Slack, or email.

- **Emojis and punctuation shape meaning** – learn to decode and use these subtle cues thoughtfully to avoid miscommunication.

- **Protect your digital energy** – set boundaries, take breaks, and manage digital noise so that communication stays meaningful, not overwhelming.

<u>Chapter 5: Practical Action Points</u>

- **Audit your digital conversations this week.** Which ones felt draining? Which felt energizing?

- **Try using someone's name and a personal detail in your next three messages.** Notice the difference.

- **Create a simple digital boundary.** It could be "No social media after 9 p.m." or "Only check messages twice a day."

- **Practice mindful messaging.** Pause before sending and reread your message. Ask: Is this clear? Respectful? In the right tone?

- **Post something positive or intentional on social media.** See how others respond when you show up with value.

CHAPTER 6

Bridging the Gap - How to Connect Across Cultures and Differences

"Strength lies in differences, not in similarities."
- Stephen R. Covey

In a world that's more connected than ever, we constantly find ourselves engaging with people from different backgrounds, cultures, and perspectives. Whether you're attending university, entering the workforce, or building a community online, one thing is certain: cultural competence is no longer optional. It's a vital communication skill for thriving in today's global environment.

This chapter is about expanding your lens. You'll learn how to navigate conversations across cultures, recognize and unlearn biases, adapt your communication style, and build inclusive social circles. The goal isn't to be perfect—it's to be curious, open, and respectful.

When you approach diversity with a willingness to learn, you grow as a communicator and as a person.

Understanding Cultural Competence

What Is Cultural Competence and Why It Matters

Cultural competence means being aware of, respectful toward, and effective in communicating with people from different cultures, identities, and experiences.

It involves a mix of knowledge (about cultures and customs), skills (like listening and adapting), and attitudes (such as empathy and humility).

Culturally competent individuals don't assume everyone thinks like they do. They ask questions, stay curious, and avoid snap judgments. Research shows that culturally competent communication improves collaboration, trust, and problem-solving in diverse groups (Betancourt et al., 2003).

Checking Your Own Biases

We all carry biases—some conscious, some unconscious. These biases are shaped by family, media, and life experiences. They're not a moral failing, but if left unchecked, they can influence how we treat others.

Try this: Reflect on the stereotypes you were exposed to growing up. Have any of them shaped how you perceive certain groups? Tools like Harvard's Implicit Association Test (IAT) can help you uncover blind spots. Awareness is the first step to change (Greenwald et al., 2009).

The Media's Role in Shaping Perception

Media plays a massive role in influencing how we view cultures and people different from us. Think critically about how certain groups are portrayed in TV, film, and social media. Are they shown in complex, human ways—or just as stereotypes?

Being media literate can help you resist bias and promote equity in your own communication.

Increasing Cultural Awareness

How to Expand Your Cultural Worldview

You don't need a passport to become culturally aware. Start with books, podcasts, and documentaries created by people from different backgrounds. Attend local cultural festivals, try new cuisines, or volunteer with diverse communities.

Exposure is key to building understanding.

Respecting Cultural Norms and Traditions

Respect starts with curiosity. Before entering a new environment—whether it's a workplace, community center, or someone's home—take time to learn about the expected behaviors, greetings, and traditions. For example, direct eye contact is a sign of confidence in some cultures, but can be seen as disrespectful in others. Small acts of awareness make a big impact.

Bridging Communication Gaps

Common Cross-Cultural Barriers

Language is the most obvious barrier, but nonverbal

communication often causes misunderstandings too. A thumbs-up gesture may be encouraging in the U.S. but offensive in other countries. Even silence, tone, and body language can mean different things depending on the context (Gudykunst, 2004).

Strategies for Clearer Communication

- **Use simple, inclusive language.** Avoid idioms, slang, and jargon that might not translate well.

- **Ask clarifying questions.** Don't pretend to understand something if you don't.

- **Utilize tools.** Google Translate, language apps, or a bilingual friend can bridge the gap.

Adapt Your Style, Don't Erase Yourself

Cultural competence isn't about changing who you are—it's about being flexible. If you speak fast and animatedly, you might need to slow down and simplify for someone new to your language. This isn't "dumbing it down" – it's meeting people where they are.

Find Common Ground

One of the easiest ways to connect is to look for what you share. Love of food, music, art, or sports often transcends language. Starting from shared interests creates a strong foundation for deeper conversation.

Let's Examine Some Real-life Examples

Let's examine two real-life examples that demonstrate finding common ground

Story 1: Sofia, Digital Pen Pals

Sofia, a 20-year-old university student in London, joined a global student exchange platform during lockdown. She got paired with Amina, a nursing student in Nairobi. Initially, their conversations were awkward.

Sofia used a lot of British slang, while Amina typed more formally.

But instead of getting discouraged, they talked about their favorite foods, childhood memories, and how they each celebrated holidays.

Sofia learned about Kenyan traditions, and Amina got curious about British pop culture. Through weekly Zoom calls and Instagram messages, their communication grew more natural.

They developed a bond built on empathy and curiosity—not just shared language.

LESSONS TO LEARN FROM SOFIA & AMINA CONNECTION:

- Sofia (UK) and Amina (Kenya) initially struggled due to language style differences and cultural unfamiliarity.

- Instead of giving up, they leaned into curiosity—sharing personal stories, favorite foods, and holiday traditions.

- Over time, they built rapport through consistent, low-pressure digital exchanges.

> **Key Takeaway:** Intentional curiosity and shared storytelling can overcome initial discomfort and build genuine cross-cultural connections—even online. This example shows how empathy and openness make global communication both possible and rewarding.

Story 2: Navigating Cultural Nuances in Workspaces

Marcus, a 24-year-old recent grad in Toronto, started an internship at a global tech company. He noticed that his colleague Hiroshi from Japan would avoid direct eye contact and rarely spoke up in meetings. At first, Marcus thought Hiroshi wasn't interested. But after reading about Japanese communication styles, he realized that Hiroshi valued harmony and indirect communication.

Marcus began using more open-ended questions and left space in conversations for Hiroshi to chime in. Eventually, they developed a strong working relationship—and Hiroshi appreciated Marcus's efforts to adapt.

LESSONS TO LEARN FROM MARCUS & HIROSHI CONNECTION:

- Marcus misinterpreted Hiroshi's indirectness and lack of eye contact as disinterest.

- He educated himself on Japanese communication norms and shifted his approach (more open-ended questions, slower pacing).

- As a result, Hiroshi felt more comfortable and the collaboration flourished.

Key Takeaway: Flexibility in communication style and cultural awareness are essential in diverse environments. When you take time to understand someone else's norms, you create space for trust, collaboration, and mutual respect.

Storytelling Across Cultures

Why Stories Connect Us

Stories are universal. They teach values, pass down history, and make us feel seen. Sharing your story—or listening to someone else's—is one of the most powerful ways to bridge cultural divides.

Crafting Culturally Respectful Stories

When sharing your story:

- Be authentic, but avoid generalizations about your own culture.

- Use relatable emotions and experiences to connect.

- Choose themes that resonate across cultures, like family, resilience, or growth.

Listening to Learn

Actively seek out stories from cultures different than your own. Listen to oral histories, watch global films, or follow international content creators. Reflect on what their stories teach you. Story exchange builds empathy and mutual respect (Chung et al., 2016).

Building Inclusive Social Circles

Why Inclusion Matters

Inclusion isn't just about inviting people in—it's about creating space where they feel welcome. Research shows that diverse groups make better decisions and innovate more effectively (Page, 2007).

Simple Ways to Be More Inclusive

- Rotate who you invite to hangouts.

- Be mindful of group dynamics: Is someone always left out?

- Use inclusive language: Avoid phrases or jokes that

exclude people based on culture, race, gender, or orientation.

Encourage Open Dialogue

Foster honest conversations in your circles. If a cultural misunderstanding happens, don't avoid it—address it with kindness. A simple,

"Hey, I didn't know that, thanks for telling me"

can go a long way.

Celebrate Differences

Make space to honor different traditions. Host cultural exchange nights, celebrate holidays from various backgrounds, or invite friends to share their customs. Celebrating diversity strengthens bonds and expands everyone's worldview.

Cultural competence isn't about knowing everything—it's about showing up with humility, curiosity, and a willingness to learn. When you take the time to understand different cultural backgrounds, you don't just become a better communicator—you become a better friend, leader, and global citizen.

In today's world, where one DM can connect you with someone halfway across the globe, your ability to engage with diverse groups is one of your greatest assets. Every thoughtful conversation, every respectful question, every shared story helps to break down barriers and build bridges. The more inclusive and open-minded you become, the richer your relationships—and your life—will be.

So keep asking questions, keep learning, and keep showing up for others with empathy. You're not just building communication skills. You're shaping a more connected, inclusive world.

Chapter 6: Key Takeaways

- **Cultural competence is a learnable skill**, rooted in curiosity, respect, and adaptability—not perfection or expertise.

- **Self-awareness is key to inclusion** – recognizing your own biases and how media influences your perceptions helps build more thoughtful communication.

- **Adaptability bridges communication gaps** – adjusting your language, pace, and tone across cultures shows empathy and fosters trust.

- **Shared stories create shared understanding** – personal storytelling and active listening across cultures build empathy and human connection.

- **Inclusive circles don't happen by accident** – intentionally invite diverse perspectives, rotate who gets a voice, and celebrate cultural traditions to create meaningful community.

Chapter 6: Practical Action Points

1. **Take the Harvard Implicit Association Test** to uncover hidden biases.

2. **Read or watch something created by a person from a culture different than your own.** Reflect on what you learned.

3. **Start a cultural exchange with a friend or classmate. Share stories or traditions.**

4. **Audit your social circle.** Does everyone look or think like you? If so, make space to connect with others outside your usual bubble.

5. **Practice inclusive communication** by avoiding slang, checking assumptions, and asking open-ended questions.

Calm the Chaos - Overcoming Social Anxiety One Step at a Time

"You don't have to control your thoughts. You just have to stop letting them control you."

- Dan Millman

Let's be honest—social anxiety sucks. It's that sweaty-palmed, heart-thudding, mind-blanking kind of fear that creeps in at the worst times. Maybe it hits when you're walking into a room full of strangers, or when your phone buzzes and you dread replying. For many young adults navigating friendships, school, jobs, or even posting online, social anxiety is a silent companion that whispers, *"Don't say the wrong thing."* But here's the truth: you're not broken, you're not alone, and you're not stuck this way.

This chapter is your roadmap to understanding and managing social anxiety, step by step. We'll explore how to recognize your unique anxiety triggers, build tools to calm your mind before a social event, reflect on interactions with clarity (not self-criticism), and use mindfulness to stay grounded. Think of this chapter as your toolkit for getting out of your head and into the moment—one meaningful connection at a time.

Identifying Triggers and Patterns

What Sets You Off?

Social anxiety doesn't just come out of nowhere—it's usually tied to specific triggers. For some, it's walking into a crowded room. For others, it's speaking up in class or making small talk with coworkers. Common triggers include:

- Large groups or unfamiliar settings

- Situations involving authority figures

- Being the center of attention

- Fear of judgment or rejection

Start tracking your experiences using a journal or notes app. After a social interaction, jot down what happened, how you felt, and what you were thinking. Over time, patterns will emerge. You'll begin to spot your anxiety's "greatest hits."

Recognizing Your Body's Clues

Anxiety shows up physically before your brain even catches on. Pay attention to:

- Increased heart rate

- Sweaty palms

- Shaky hands or voice

- Dry mouth

- Tight chest

And don't forget emotional and cognitive signs like irritability, overthinking, or expecting the worst. These are all valid signals. Becoming aware of them helps you catch anxiety early—and manage it before it spirals.

Reflection Exercise: Rewind and Learn

Take 10 minutes to reflect on your last uncomfortable social interaction. Ask yourself:

- What was the situation?

- How did I feel before, during, and after?

- What did I tell myself in that moment?

- What went better than I thought?

This isn't about beating yourself up—it's about understanding your anxiety so you can face it head-on next time.

Strategies for Managing Pre-Social Event Anxiety

Your Pre-Event Ritual

Think of preparing for a social event like prepping for a big game. You wouldn't just show up without warming up. Create a calming pre-event ritual:

- Breathe deeply (inhale for 4, hold for 4, exhale for 4)

- Listen to music that lifts your mood

- Do a light stretch or walk to release tension

This tells your brain, "We've got this."

Set Small, Doable Goals

Social success doesn't mean being the loudest in the room. It might mean:

- Saying hi to one new person

- Asking one question in a group

- Staying at an event for 30 minutes

Setting flexible, realistic goals reduces pressure and gives you a sense of accomplishment. Research supports this too—small goals are proven to reduce anxiety and boost self-efficacy (Bandura, 1997).

Use Visualization and Affirmations

Before your next social event, close your eyes and picture the best-case scenario: You walk in with confidence. You smile. Someone smiles back. You talk, laugh, feel good. Visualization activates the same neural pathways as real-life experiences (Holmes & Mathews, 2010), making it easier to recreate success.

That said, it's worth noting that visualization doesn't work the same for everyone. For some people—especially those prone to negative intrusive thoughts—visualizing positive outcomes can occasionally trigger more anxiety if not guided carefully. If that happens, try using visualization alongside grounding techniques or seek structured support (like guided visualizations or coaching). Most importantly, approach it with curiosity, not pressure.

Pair this with affirmations like:

- *"I can handle this."*

- *"It's okay to be myself."*

- *"One conversation at a time."*

Say them while you get ready, during your commute, or in your head before walking in.

Have a Conversation Toolkit

Feeling stuck on what to say? Prep a few go-to topics:

- *"Have you been to one of these events before?"*

- *"What do you usually do on weekends?"*

- *"I love your [accessory/shirt/etc.]—where'd you get it?"*

These openers are simple but effective. Keep 3–5 of them in your mental back pocket.

Post-Interaction Reflection Techniques

Review Without the Self-Hate

After a social event, it's easy to replay every awkward pause or joke that didn't land. Instead of spiraling, try this:

1. What went well?

2. What did I learn?

3. What would I try differently next time?

You're building skills, not aiming for perfection.

Journal the Feelings

Write about how you felt emotionally and physically. Did you notice less tension than usual? Were your thoughts more encouraging? Noting progress, even small wins, reinforces positive change.

Celebrate Your Wins

Did you show up? Speak up? Stay longer than planned? That counts. Create a "Confidence Jar" where you write each win on a slip of paper and keep them in a jar. On tough days, read them back to yourself.

Reframe Rejection

Someone didn't engage? You stumbled on your words? That's okay. Rejection isn't failure—it's feedback. Practice telling yourself:

- *"That didn't go as planned, but I'm proud I tried."*

- *"I'm growing every time I show up."*

Mindfulness Practices for Social Situations

Why Mindfulness Works

Mindfulness helps reduce anxiety by bringing your attention to the present. You're not stuck in past regrets or future worries—you're right here, right now. Studies show mindfulness significantly lowers social anxiety symptoms and improves emotional regulation (Goldin & Gross, 2010).

Practice Mindful Breathing

- Try this before entering a social space:

- Inhale deeply through your nose for 4 seconds

- Pause (or hold your breath) for 4 seconds before exhaling

- Exhale slowly through your mouth for 4 seconds

- Repeat 3–5 times

This simple breath pattern activates your parasympathetic nervous system, which is the part of your autonomic nervous system responsible for calming the body after stress or danger. When activated, it slows your heart rate, lowers blood pressure, and sends signals to your brain that you're safe. This can counteract the "fight or flight" response triggered by social anxiety and help you feel more grounded and present (Porges, 2011).

While "fight or flight" is commonly used to describe the body's stress reaction, it's important to note that many people—especially those with social anxiety—experience a third response: "freeze." This is the sensation of going blank, freezing up, or feeling paralyzed during social or public situations. It's not a sign of weakness; it's the nervous system's attempt to protect you from perceived danger. Recognizing freeze responses as part of the stress cycle (fight, flight, or freeze) can help you respond with more self-compassion and targeted calming strategies.

Mindful Observation

Once you're in the space, gently observe without judgment:

- Notice the colors around you

- Listen to the sounds in the room

- Feel your feet on the ground

This grounds you and reduces racing thoughts.

Be Present in Conversations

When speaking with someone, focus fully on them:

- Make eye contact

- Listen to their words without rehearsing your reply

- Nod or respond with small affirmations like *"I see,"* or *"That makes sense."*

This not only calms you—it makes the other person feel heard and valued.

Social anxiety doesn't define you—it's something you can work through. With the right tools and mindset, every conversation becomes a little easier. Keep showing up for yourself. Progress lives in the small wins. Let's keep building.

Chapter 7: Key Takeaways

- **Awareness is your first tool**—tracking your physical, emotional, and thought-based triggers helps you recognize patterns and regain control.

- **Preparation builds confidence**—use calming rituals, visualization, affirmations, and small social goals to set yourself up for success.

- **Reflection fuels growth**—review interactions with compassion, not criticism, and celebrate every small win as meaningful progress.

- **Mindfulness grounds you in the moment**—breathwork and present-moment awareness calm the body and help you show up fully in conversations.

- **You're not defined by anxiety**—you're building resilience one conversation, one breath, and one brave step at a time.

<u>Chapter 7: Practical Action Points</u>

1. **Start an Anxiety Trigger Journal**: Track your patterns, thoughts, and wins.

2. **Create a Pre-Event Ritual**: Use breathwork, music, or movement to center yourself.

3. **Use Visualization and Affirmations**: Prep your mindset like an athlete before a game.

4. **Reflect and Celebrate**: After each social event, journal what went well.

5. **Practice Mindfulness Daily**: Use simple breathing or grounding exercises.

Your Words Matter!

Can you believe how far you've come already?

You're nearly halfway through your journey to becoming an extraordinary communicator. You've discovered tools to navigate digital interactions, strategies to handle tough conversations, and ways to connect authentically across diverse settings. You've learned the power of empathy, active listening, and clear self-expression—and this is just the beginning.

But imagine someone out there, right now, who's struggling exactly as you once did. They're overwhelmed by social anxiety, unsure of how to express themselves clearly, or simply looking for confidence in their communication. Your experience and insights, even at this midpoint, can offer them hope, encouragement, and direction.

Your review can change someone's trajectory right now.

If you've found value, clarity, or inspiration in what you've learned so far, please consider sharing your thoughts. Your words could be exactly what someone else needs to keep going.

Please help a young adult by leaving this book an honest review.

By leaving your review, you'll:

- Encourage others to start their own journey toward confident communication.

- Provide practical insights that help others see what's possible.

- Contribute to creating a community of empowered, skilled communicators.

Here's how you can make a difference:
Simply scan the QR code or Click the link below to leave your review:

Scan to Leave a review

Share your thoughts—it takes less than a minute!

Your perspective truly matters. Let's keep building a world filled with confident, authentic, and empowered communicators.

Thank you from the bottom of my heart. Your support means the world to me. Now, let's get back to leveling up your communication skills.

— Your biggest fan, Roshel Waite

CHAPTER 8

Speak Like You Mean It - Public Speaking Without the Panic

"They may forget what you said, but they will never forget how you made them feel."

- Maya Angelou

Picture yourself standing in front of a crowd, the spotlight on you, and all eyes waiting for your words. Your palms sweat, your heart pounds, and your mind races through everything you planned to say. Whether it's a class presentation, a meeting at work, or speaking at a community event, public speaking can be nerve-wracking. But here's the truth: with the right tools, structure, and mindset, you can deliver a message that not only informs but inspires.

This chapter is designed to give you a solid foundation in public speaking—from crafting a message that resonates to owning the stage with presence and confidence. We'll break down structure, body language, visualization, storytelling, and actionable steps so that when your moment comes, you're more than ready.

Structuring Your Message for Impact

A powerful presentation starts with a clear and compelling structure. Structure gives your message shape and flow. It's how you guide your audience from curiosity to clarity—and it's often what separates forgettable talks from memorable ones.

Why Structure Matters

A logical structure helps your audience stay engaged and remember your message. Research suggests that structured presentations improve comprehension and retention, as the brain processes organized information more efficiently.

Psychologists and communication experts agree that a clear structure helps your audience follow the flow and stay engaged—especially when learning new or complex material.

Think of it like this: If your speech is a journey, structure is the map. Without it, your audience can get lost. Without a map, your audience ends up guessing where the speech is going—and once they're lost, you've lost them.

When you give people a path, they follow it with confidence—and that confidence builds connection.

The Three-Part Framework

1. **Introduction**: Begin with a strong hook—a personal story, a question, or a surprising fact to hook attention. Clearly state your purpose and build a bridge to your audience's interests. An intro like this outlines what the audience can expect.

2. **Body**: Break your content into 2–4 main points. Each point should flow logically into the next. Use signposting language like "first," "next," or "on the other hand" to guide your audience. Repetition and real-world examples reinforce understanding.

3. **Conclusion**: Wrap up by summarizing your main points and delivering a compelling takeaway. Whether it's a call-to-action, a story, or a challenge, leave your audience with something to remember.

Common Frameworks

- Problem-Solution: Begin by outlining a problem and then present your solution. This framework is persuasive and effective when you're trying to motivate action.

- Chronological: Tell a story or explain steps in a timeline. Perfect for personal narratives or process explanations.

- Thematic: Group similar ideas into themes to simplify complex information.

Tailoring to Your Audience

Consider who you're speaking to. Are they peers, professionals, or people unfamiliar with your topic? Adjust your vocabulary, depth, and tone to meet their needs.

A presentation on digital entrepreneurship for Gen Z should sound and look very different from a talk to a room of senior executives.

Audience analysis helps shape everything from your examples to your humor.

Harnessing Body Language for Persuasive Speaking

Your words matter—but so does how you deliver them. In emotional communication—especially when words and tone don't match—nonverbal cues like body language and tone of voice can account for over half the message, according to Albert Mehrabian's research (1972). Mehrabian's model only applies to conveying feelings or attitudes—not facts, instructions, or technical content.

In public speaking, your voice and body language can enhance (or dilute) your message, especially when expressing emotions.

Confident body language enhances credibility, while nervous movements can distract.

The Power of Gestures

Use your hands to highlight key points. Gestures are the visual punctuation of your message. They signal emphasis, rhythm, and emotion. Don't overdo it—excessive or erratic movement can come off as nervous energy. But standing stiffly can make you appear disconnected. Practice your gestures so they feel fluid and natural.

Posture and Presence

Your posture tells the audience how confident you are—before you even speak. Stand tall, shoulders relaxed, feet shoulder-width apart. Avoid slouching, crossing your arms, or shifting from foot to foot. Strong posture not only projects confidence, but also allows you to breathe better and project your voice more effectively.

Reading the Room

Your audience gives feedback—even when silent. Are they leaning in and nodding? That's engagement. Are they checking their phones or shifting uncomfortably? That's a cue to adjust. Maybe ask a question, change your tone, or involve the audience with a quick anecdote or story.

PRACTICE EXERCISE

Record yourself speaking for 2–3 minutes. Focus on your gestures, posture, and movement. Are your nonverbal cues matching your message? Are you stiff, overly animated, or disengaged? Notice any distracting habits. Adjust and re-record. Practicing on video can reveal what mirrors often don't.

Visualization Techniques for Stage Confidence

Elite athletes and performers use visualization to mentally rehearse success—and so can you.

Why Visualization Works

Visualization activates the same neural pathways as real-life experiences. In a study by Taylor & Pham (1996), students who visualized themselves engaging in the process of studying—rather than just visualizing success—performed significantly better. This shows that visualizing the steps you'll take—not just the outcome—can lead to better performance and reduce pre-task anxiety.

When you visualize success, you train your brain to anticipate it.

Create a Visualization Routine

- Find a quiet space and close your eyes.

- Picture yourself walking onto the stage or up to the podium.

- Imagine yourself delivering your opening lines with clarity and ease.

- Visualize the audience reacting positively—nodding, smiling, applauding.

The more sensory detail you include (sight, sound, even smell), the more effective the visualization becomes. Even five minutes of visualization before speaking can reduce anxiety and boost performance.

Combine with Rehearsal

Pair visualization with real practice. Say your speech out loud. Combine mental rehearsal with physical delivery to strengthen your performance from both angles.

Engaging Your Audience with Storytelling

Facts tell. Stories sell. A compelling story can turn a decent speech into a powerful one.

The Psychology of Stories

Our brains are wired for stories. Neuroscientific research shows that storytelling activates multiple areas of the brain, increasing empathy and retention (Zak, 2014).

Crafting a Story

Use the three-act structure:

- **Beginning**: Set the scene

- **Middle**: Introduce conflict or tension

- **End**: Resolve the story with a clear message

Choose personal stories or relatable anecdotes that support your key point.

Balancing Data and Narrative

Start with a story to build emotional connection, then back it up with data. This combo keeps your audience engaged while building your credibility.

Example

Instead of saying, *"85% of young adults feel anxious speaking in public,"* begin with:

> "In high school, I once faked a stomach ache to skip a class presentation. Just the thought of standing in front of my peers made my stomach flip. Years later, I've learned strategies that made all the difference—and I want to share them with you today."

Then follow up with the statistic.

Public speaking isn't just about impressing others—it's about connecting, sharing, and leading. With practice, structure, and a little storytelling magic, you'll discover that you have something powerful to say—and the voice to say it with impact.

Chapter 8: Key Takeaways

- **A strong structure is the backbone of every great speech** – use a clear intro, logical body, and memorable conclusion to guide your audience with clarity.

- **Nonverbal communication matters** – confident posture, gestures, and audience awareness amplify your message and build trust.

- **Visualization primes your mind for success** – mental rehearsal can ease nerves and strengthen stage presence when paired with real practice.

- **Stories engage, data supports** – start with relatable narratives to connect emotionally, then follow up with facts to inform and persuade.

- **Public speaking is a skill, not a talent** – with preparation, reflection, and the right tools, anyone can inspire an audience.

Chapter 8: Practical Action Points

1. **Choose a Speech Framework**: Try problem-solution or chronological for your next presentation.

2. **Script and Outline**: Don't memorize word-for-word, but know your main points.

3. **Record and Review**: Practice in front of a mirror or record yourself to fine-tune delivery.

4. **Visualize Success**: Spend five minutes visualizing a confident, engaging performance.

5. **Use One Personal Story**: Pick a short story to humanize your message and connect with your audience.

CHAPTER 9
Respectfully Bold - The Art of Assertiveness and Setting Boundaries

"Daring to set boundaries is about having the courage to love ourselves, even when we risk disappointing others."

- Brené Brown

Imagine this: you're in a conversation, someone interrupts you repeatedly, talks over your ideas, or even dismisses your input entirely. Your chest tightens. You want to speak up—but you freeze, unsure of how to say what you feel without sounding rude or causing conflict. This is where assertiveness steps in. It's not about shouting louder or dominating others—it's about standing tall in your truth, while still respecting the space others occupy.

Assertiveness represents a balanced communication style between passivity and aggression. It allows you to express your thoughts, needs, and boundaries clearly and respectfully. In the digital age, where tone can be misinterpreted and boundaries are easily crossed online and offline, assertiveness becomes an essential life skill—especially for young adults navigating independence, work, school, and relationships.

Recognizing the Difference Between Assertiveness and Aggression

Assertiveness and aggression may sometimes appear similar on the surface—both involve speaking up. But the *intention* and *impact* behind them are vastly different. Assertiveness is rooted in mutual respect: for yourself and for others. It's about clarity, confidence, and consideration. Aggression, on the other hand, often disregards the other person's feelings, focusing instead on winning or controlling the conversation. It can come off as hostile, overbearing, or even intimidating.

Here's the difference in action:

- **Assertive**: *"I feel frustrated when meetings start late. Can we agree on a consistent time?"*

- **Aggressive**: *"You're always late—do you even care about other people's time?"*

See the difference? One invites collaboration and solution-finding; the other assigns blame and escalates tension. According to the Mayo Clinic, assertive communication can boost self-esteem, reduce stress, and foster healthier relationships, while aggressive communication tends to escalate conflict and damage trust.

Learning to recognize aggressive tendencies in yourself is just as important as identifying them in others. Common signals of aggression include speaking with a raised voice, using sarcasm or put-downs, monopolizing conversations, interrupting frequently, or using accusatory language like "you never" or "you always."

The key to assertiveness is expressing your truth without steamrolling someone else's.

The Benefits of Assertive Communication

Assertiveness isn't just a helpful communication tool—it's a mindset that positively impacts every area of your life. When you communicate assertively, you're acknowledging that your needs and opinions are valid while also showing that you value others'. This dual-respect approach enhances interpersonal relationships, builds trust, and cultivates mutual understanding.

Research supports this. A 2018 review published in *Clinical Psychology: Science and Practice* emphasized that assertiveness training is a well-established, evidence-based approach that improves self-esteem, reduces anxiety, and strengthens relationships (Speed, Goldstein, & Goldfried, 2018). Despite its proven effectiveness, it's often overlooked in modern therapy and education—a gap that's especially relevant for young adults navigating high-pressure environments.

One young adult shared that after learning assertive communication, she was finally able to tell her parents that she needed space and independence—something she'd always felt too guilty to express.

Another recounted how advocating for himself in a toxic work environment helped shift the dynamics and even inspired coworkers to speak up too. Assertiveness allows you to stop people-pleasing and start self-respecting.

Assertive people are more likely to:

- Set healthy boundaries and avoid burnout

- Experience less anxiety and resentment

- Build stronger, more authentic relationships

Many young adults have shared how transforming their communication style changed their lives. For example, one college student said that learning to speak up respectfully in group projects helped her gain more leadership roles and be taken seriously by peers. Another shared how setting boundaries with family improved their mental health and independence.

Strategies for Cultivating Assertiveness

Like any skill, assertiveness takes practice. Start with these steps:

- **Use "I" Statements**: When you say "**I feel...**" or "**I need...**" you're focusing on your experience instead of blaming others. For example: "I feel overwhelmed when I'm added to projects last-minute. Can we discuss upcoming tasks earlier?"

- **Start Small**: Begin by asserting yourself in less intimidating settings—like ordering food exactly how you want it, or voicing your preferences in a group chat. Gradually work your way up to more emotionally charged conversations.

- **Stay Calm and Composed.** Your body language Matters. Keep an open stance, maintain eye contact, and use a calm, even tone. If your words say one thing but your body language says another, your message can become muddled. Regulate your tone and body language. Assertiveness is strongest when it comes from a grounded place.

- **Rehearse**: Try writing down what you want to say and practicing it aloud. Role-playing scenarios with a friend can prepare you for real-life moments when clarity and confidence matter most.

- **Self-Coach**: After every assertive moment (no matter how small), take note of how it felt. What worked? What didn't? This reflection sharpens your awareness and helps refine your style over time.

- **Role-Play Scenarios**: Practice with a friend or in front of a mirror. It helps to rehearse how you'll assert yourself in tricky situations. Practice in Low-Stakes Settings. Start by expressing your preferences with friends or during casual conversations.

Techniques for Setting Clear Boundaries

Boundaries are the invisible lines that define what you are and aren't comfortable with. They help preserve your emotional and physical energy and protect your peace.

Yet, many of us struggle with setting or enforcing them, especially when we fear being judged, rejected, or seen as difficult.

Boundaries exist in many forms. Think about different areas where boundaries matter:

- **Time**: Protecting your schedule from overcommitment by saying *no* to last-minute plans when you're overwhelmed.

- **Space**: Needing privacy or alone time. For instance, asking roommates to knock before entering your room.

- **Emotional**: Refusing to engage in conversations that feel manipulative or disrespectful.

- **Digital**: Managing social media boundaries, setting screen time limits, muting notifications, or choosing not to respond immediately. Protecting your privacy and mental clarity online is just as important.

Use this quick formula to express a boundary:

"When [specific behavior] happens, I feel [emotion]. What I need is [boundary]."

For example: *"When I'm interrupted, I feel frustrated. What I need is a chance to finish my thought."* or *"When messages come in after 10 p.m., I feel overwhelmed. I need to unplug in the evenings to get good rest."*

Effective boundaries must also be upheld. If someone violates a limit, calmly and clearly reinforce it. If necessary, establish consequences (e.g. leaving the conversation). You deserve to be in relationships where your boundaries are honored.

> **Key Takeaway**: Setting boundaries is a form of self-respect. Boundaries let others know what's acceptable and what isn't. Without them, we risk resentment, burnout, and poor relationship dynamics.

Navigating Difficult Conversations with Confidence

Difficult conversations are unavoidable—but they're also necessary. Whether it's confronting a friend, giving feedback to a coworker, or addressing a toxic dynamic—it's how we handle these moments that defines our maturity. Since difficult conversations are inevitable, use them to clarify misunderstandings, heal relationships, and reset expectations. Avoiding them only prolongs discomfort and builds resentment.

How to prepare for a difficult conversation.

Before the conversation:

- **Set an Intention**: What do you hope to achieve? Keep it focused and constructive.

- **Practice Self-Regulation**: Use grounding techniques like deep breathing, stretching, or journaling.

- **Choose the Right Place**: Avoid triggering environments or moments of high stress.

- **Choose Your Timing**: Avoid bringing up sensitive topics in stressful or rushed moments.

During the conversation:

- Use "I" Statements: *"I noticed..."* instead of *"You always..."*. Stick to facts rather than accusations.

- Reflect back what you hear to show you're listening and open to understanding the other person's point of view. *"So what I'm hearing is..."*

- Be open to feedback. Conversations are two-way streets. Avoid Escalating Language. Keep your tone even and body language open.

If emotions run high and things get heated, pause the discussion. Say, *"Let's take a break and come back to this."* or *"I need a moment to regroup. Can we revisit this in an hour?"* Taking breaks allows both people to return with more clarity. Emotional regulation during conflict is a power skill. As the Gottman Institute suggests, taking breaks during difficult conversations improves long-term resolution outcomes (Gottman & Gottman, 2015).

After the conversation, follow up. Clarify what was agreed upon and check in emotionally. Did both parties feel heard? Is any follow-up needed? This step helps solidify trust and make sure you're on the same page.

Respectful Disagreement and Conflict Resolution

Disagreements don't have to be confrontational. In fact, they can strengthen relationships if handled with openness and empathy. Respectful disagreement involves curiosity, emotional control, and the willingness to hear different perspectives.

Here's how:

- **Stay Curious and Ask Questions**: "Can you tell me more about how you see it?" or *"Help me understand where you're coming from."*

- **Stay Calm**: Avoid raising your voice or using defensive body language.

- **Validate Their Perspective and Acknowledge Their Feelings**: Validation isn't agreement—it's acknowledgment. Say, *"I see this matters to you, and I appreciate you sharing it."*

- **Look for Common Ground**: You might not agree on everything, but can you agree on the goal?

Conflict resolution isn't about "winning." It's about mutual understanding. One effective model is the win-win approach, where both parties express their needs and work toward a shared solution. The idea of a win-win resolution is widely used in negotiation and was popularized by Stephen Covey in *The 7 Habits of Highly Effective People.*

As many coaches say, disagreement can be viewed as data—it reveals values, priorities, and areas for clarification. Conflicts, when handled well, can be catalysts for growth. They help you understand others, refine your boundaries, and communicate more effectively. The goal isn't to avoid tension—it's to learn how to move through it with integrity.

Remember: Conflict isn't a sign of failure—it's a sign that two people care enough to engage. The goal isn't to avoid disagreement; it's to handle it with grace.

Assertiveness and boundaries are not just about communication—they're about honoring your needs, preserving your energy, and showing others how to treat you. They are key to thriving in both digital and real-world relationships. With consistent practice, you'll find your voice—and use it with strength and respect.

Chapter 9: Key Takeaways

- **Assertiveness is balanced communication**—it's about expressing your needs clearly while respecting others, not dominating or withdrawing.

- **Boundaries are acts of self-respect**—they protect your time, energy, and emotions and should be communicated calmly, clearly, and consistently.

- **Use "I" statements to speak your truth**—focus on your experience rather than blaming, and rehearse your message in advance when needed.

- **Difficult conversations are opportunities for growth**—prepare with intention, stay emotionally grounded, and follow up with empathy and clarity.

- **Respectful disagreement strengthens trust**—staying curious, calm, and collaborative turns conflict into deeper understanding, not division.

Chapter 9: Practical Action Points

1. **Audit Your Communication Style**: Track moments this week where you spoke up—or didn't. What patterns do you notice?

2. **Write and Rehearse a Boundary Statement**: Pick one area of your life where you need a boundary and practice asserting it.

3. **Prepare for a Challenging Conversation**: Choose a topic you've been avoiding and write a script to approach it with assertiveness.

4. **Watch for Aggression Triggers**: Notice when you get reactive. Practice pausing, breathing, and reframing before responding.

5. **Celebrate Your Progress**: Each time you advocate for yourself with respect, write it down. This builds momentum and reinforces your new skills.

CHAPTER 10

Networking with Purpose - Building Relationships That Matter

"The currency of real networking is not greed but generosity."

- Keith Ferrazzi

I magine walking into a room full of strangers at a conference. Everyone is talking, laughing, exchanging business cards. You freeze for a second, unsure who to approach or what to say. Should you jump into a conversation or wait for someone to talk to you? Networking can feel intimidating, especially for young adults entering the professional world for the first time.

But here's the truth: networking isn't about being the most outgoing person in the room. It's about building genuine connections—relationships rooted in mutual value, curiosity, and authenticity. And when done well, it can open doors you didn't even know existed.

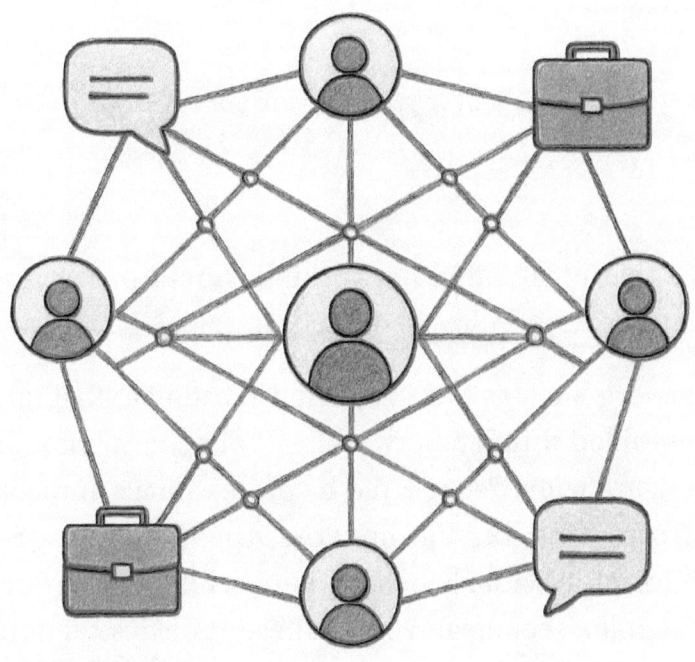

The Art of Networking: Building Genuine Connections

Let's start by redefining what networking really is. It's not about collecting as many contacts as possible or handing out business cards like flyers. It's about establishing meaningful, mutually beneficial relationships. Think of it less like a job interview and more like making a new friend with professional overlap. Relational networking, unlike transactional networking, isn't about what someone can do for you today—it's about creating relationships that grow and evolve over time.

In fact, many job opportunities and collaborations happen through these organic connections. One young designer shared that after a casual chat at a co-working space, she landed her first freelance client—who later became a long-term mentor. It all started with:

> **"Hey, I love your laptop stickers—are you in design too?"**

It's proof that meaningful networking is built on curiosity and shared interests, not rehearsed pitches.

Career experts such as Matt Youngquist, estimate that up to 85% of jobs are filled through networking (Youngquist, cited in NPR, 2009), a figure widely supported by professionals and echoed in LinkedIn career insights. Furthermore, Apollo Technical reported that 80% of professionals believe networking is vital for career success (Apollo Technical, 2023). These statistics reinforce how essential building authentic professional relationships really is.

Identifying Networking Opportunities

Networking opportunities aren't limited to formal events like conferences or job fairs. They can happen anywhere—at community events, volunteer gatherings, or even on social media platforms. The key is to stay open and observant. If you're at a workshop, introduce yourself to the person sitting next to you. If you're online, engage thoughtfully in LinkedIn discussions or comment on someone's post with genuine insights. Every interaction is a chance to learn, connect, and expand your circle.

Developing a Networking Mindset

Approach networking with a mindset of giving, not just getting. Ask questions like:

- How can I help this person?

- What value can I offer?

When you lead with curiosity and generosity, your connections naturally deepen. Some ways to do this include recommending a helpful resource, introducing them to someone in your network, or simply showing interest in their work. This mindset shift makes networking feel less awkward and more human. Research supports this: people embedded in strong social networks are more likely to find employment and experience career mobility (Granovetter, 1973/1995). Granovetter's classic research showed that **'weak ties'** - acquaintances rather than close friends—are often the key bridges to new job opportunities and upward mobility.

Building Rapport and Trust

Rapport is built through active listening, shared experiences, and mutual respect. Start conversations with open-ended questions like,

> *"What inspired you to get into this field?"*

or

> *"What's a recent project you've enjoyed working on?"*

Use body language to show you're engaged—nod, maintain eye contact, and smile genuinely. Trust is also built through consistency and follow-through. If you promise to share a link or follow up, do it. These small actions show reliability, which is the foundation of professional trust.

Leveraging LinkedIn and Professional Platforms

Social media isn't just for memes and selfies. Platforms like LinkedIn can be powerful tools for building your professional brand and expanding your network. But success on LinkedIn isn't about shouting your achievements—it's about telling your professional story in a way that resonates.

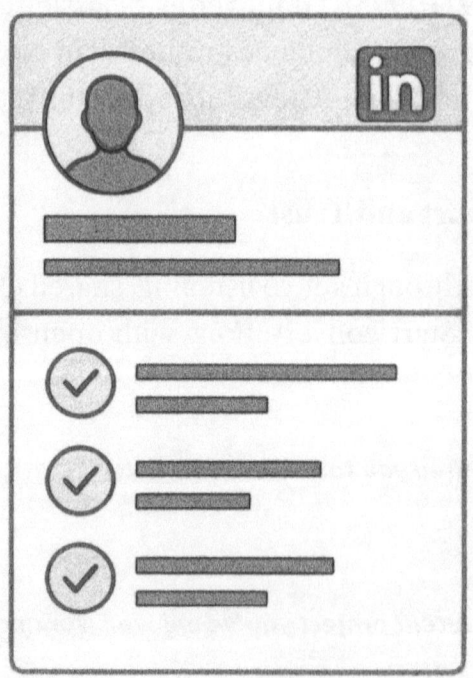

Optimizing Your Professional Profile

Think of your LinkedIn profile as your digital handshake. Your headline should go beyond your job title—it should showcase what you do and who you help.

FOR EXAMPLE:

"Marketing Student | Helping brands grow through creative storytelling" is more engaging than "Marketing Intern."

In your summary, highlight your passions, achievements, and goals. Use bullet points to make it easy to read. Include measurable results if possible, like "Grew Instagram engagement by 40% in 3 months." These specifics show your impact and help you stand out.

According to Jobvite (2022) and other recruiting studies, a large majority of recruiters—over 85%—use LinkedIn to research job candidates, making it a crucial space to represent yourself clearly and professionally.

Engaging with Your Network

Staying active on LinkedIn is about participation, not promotion. Share articles, write posts about your learning experiences, or comment on others' content with thoughtful takeaways. When you add value to conversations, people notice—and remember you.

Posts with images receive 2x the engagement compared to text-only posts (LinkedIn Marketing Solutions, 2021). Engagement builds visibility and expands your reach.

Utilizing LinkedIn Features for Networking

Join industry-specific LinkedIn groups to connect with like-minded professionals. When sending connection requests, personalize your message:

> **"Hi Alex, I enjoyed your recent article on UX design. I'd love to connect and learn more about your work."**

These small touches make a big difference.

Endorsements and recommendations are another way to build credibility. Ask peers, professors, or past employers to write a short recommendation that highlights your strengths. Offer to return the favor—it strengthens the bond and shows appreciation.

Crafting an Elevator Pitch that Resonates

An elevator pitch is your verbal business card. It's a 30-second introduction that captures who you are, what you do, and what makes you unique. Whether you're at a job fair, a networking event, or meeting someone new online, a strong pitch can make a lasting impression.

The Purpose of an Elevator Pitch

Imagine you step into an elevator with the CEO of your dream company. You've got 30 seconds to introduce yourself before the doors open. That's the power of an elevator pitch—it helps you communicate your value clearly and quickly.

Elements of a Powerful Elevator Pitch

A great pitch includes:

- A clear introduction: *"Hi, I'm Jordan, a recent graduate in environmental science."*

- A unique value proposition: *"I specialize in creating sustainable solutions for urban spaces."*

- A hook or call to action: *"I'd love to connect and share how I reduced water waste in my last internship by 25%."*

Make it personal and relevant. Avoid buzzwords and jargon—speak like a human, not a resume.

Tailoring Your Pitch for Different Audiences

Your pitch should change depending on who you're speaking to. If you're talking to a recruiter, focus on skills and achievements. If it's a peer, highlight shared interests or goals. Practice modifying your pitch to suit different contexts—it shows awareness and adaptability.

Practicing and Perfecting Delivery

Practice makes polished. Rehearse your pitch with a friend or record yourself and watch the playback. Notice your tone, pace, and body language. You want to come across as confident, but not rehearsed. The goal is to sound natural and engaging.

Follow-Up Strategies that Strengthen Bonds

Meeting someone is just the beginning—following up is where real networking happens. A thoughtful follow-up message shows appreciation, reinforces your interest, and keeps the conversation going.

The Importance of Follow-Up in

Networking People are busy. A timely follow-up helps you stay top of mind. According to a 2018 survey by LinkedIn, 70% of professionals were more likely to engage with someone who followed up within 48 hours of meeting them.

Crafting Personalized Follow-Up Messages

Your follow-up should reference something specific from your conversation.

FOR EXAMPLE:

> **"Hi Maya, I enjoyed chatting about content strategy at yesterday's panel. I checked out that podcast you mentioned—so insightful! Let's keep in touch."**

This message shows you were engaged, and it invites future interaction.

Leveraging Various Follow-Up Methods

Email is great for formal contacts, while social media or even handwritten notes can feel more personal. Choose the method that best suits your relationship. Keep it professional, but let your personality shine through.

Maintaining Long-Term Professional Relationships

Relationships need nurturing. Schedule periodic check-ins, share articles they might find useful, or congratulate them on career milestones. Even a simple "Hey, I saw this and thought of you!" message can keep the connection alive.

Organize your contacts and make reminders to touch base. This isn't about being transactional—it's about staying connected in a genuine, low-pressure way.

Networking and professional communication aren't just tools for career growth—they're essential life skills. They open doors, spark opportunities, and create a web of relationships that can support, challenge, and elevate you. With practice, intention, and authenticity, you'll become someone who doesn't just make contacts—but creates lasting connections that matter.

Chapter 10: Key Takeaways

- **Networking is about quality, not quantity** – build genuine, mutually beneficial relationships rooted in curiosity, value, and authenticity.

- **Approach every interaction with generosity** – lead with "How can I help?" rather than "What can I get?"

- **Your online presence matters** – optimize your LinkedIn profile, post thoughtfully, and personalize connection requests to build credibility.

- **Craft a flexible elevator pitch** – speak clearly about who you are, what you do, and what value you offer, tailoring your message for different audiences.

- **Follow-up builds the relationship** – reach out within 48 hours, reference shared moments, and keep connections warm through ongoing engagement.

Chapter 10: Practical Action Points

1. **Build Your Elevator Pitch**: Write and practice your 30-second introduction. Record yourself and adjust until it feels natural.

2. **Optimize Your LinkedIn Profile**: Update your headline, summary, and experience. Ask for two recommendations this week.

3. **Attend One Networking Event**: Choose a virtual or in-person event aligned with your interests. Set a goal to introduce yourself to three people.

4. **Follow Up**: After your next networking interaction, send a thoughtful follow-up message within 48 hours.

5. **Engage Online**: Comment on three LinkedIn posts this week with genuine insights. It's an easy way to build visibility and connections.

CHAPTER 11

From Acquaintances to Allies - How to Create Lasting Connections

"The most important thing in communication is hearing what isn't said."

- Peter Drucker

There's something incredibly powerful about feeling deeply understood by someone. It's the kind of connection that doesn't just happen overnight—it's nurtured, built on trust, mutual understanding, and emotional depth. In this chapter, we'll explore how to create and sustain meaningful connections with others, not just through words, but through emotional intelligence, vulnerability, and consistent communication. Whether it's a close friendship, romantic relationship, or professional alliance, these principles can help you deepen your bonds and build relationships that last.

Understanding Emotional Intelligence in Relationships

What Is Emotional Intelligence? Emotional intelligence (EI) is your ability to understand and manage your own emotions while also recognizing and responding to the emotions of others. Coined by psychologist Daniel Goleman (1995), EI includes five core components: self-awareness, self-regulation, motivation, empathy, and social skills. High emotional intelligence allows you to communicate more effectively, resolve conflicts more smoothly, and build stronger, more authentic relationships.

Why EI Matters in Relationships

Imagine having a heated disagreement with a friend. Without emotional intelligence, you might react defensively or say something you regret. But with EI, you can pause, recognize your emotional triggers, and respond calmly. You can empathize with their point of view and seek common ground. This emotional awareness not only diffuses tension but also builds trust and mutual respect. Research shows that emotional intelligence is a strong predictor of relationship satisfaction. Brackett et al. (2006) published a study titled *"Emotional Intelligence and Relationship Quality Among Couples"* in Personality and Individual Differences. The study showed that higher emotional intelligence—especially in men—was linked to higher relationship satisfaction for both partners.

Strengthening Emotional Intelligence

Start with self-awareness. Use tools like journaling or mindfulness to become more conscious of how you react in different situations. Practice self-regulation by pausing before you respond to emotional triggers. Develop empathy by actively listening to others without judgment. Try to see situations from their perspective. Engage in social skills training—practice assertive communication, resolve conflicts constructively, and express appreciation regularly. These aren't one-time skills but ongoing practices that improve the quality of every relationship.

Building Trust Through Consistent Communication

Why Trust Is Everything

Trust is the glue that holds relationships together. Without it, communication breaks down and misunderstandings multiply. Trust forms when words align with actions over time. It's built in everyday interactions—by being reliable, keeping promises, and showing up, even in small ways.

How to Build and Maintain Trust

One of the most effective ways to build trust is through consistent, transparent communication. That means speaking honestly, even when it's uncomfortable, and making space for others to do the same. Regular check-ins—whether they're daily texts or weekly coffee chats—help maintain a sense of connection. When conflict arises, lean into the discomfort instead of avoiding it. Own your mistakes, apologize sincerely, and take responsibility for your role.

Rebuilding Trust After It's Broken

Rebuilding trust takes time and consistent effort. Start by acknowledging the breach honestly. Avoid defensiveness and focus on how your actions impacted the other person. Express a genuine desire to make things right and follow through with changes. Trust isn't restored through words alone—it's proven through consistent behavior over time.

The Role of Vulnerability in Deepening Connections

The Strength in Vulnerability

We often think of vulnerability as a weakness, but it's actually one of our greatest strengths. When you allow yourself to be seen—flaws, fears, and all—you create space for deeper intimacy. Dr. Brené Brown, a leading researcher on vulnerability, found that vulnerability is the birthplace of love, belonging, and joy (Brown, 2012). Sharing your struggles and imperfections invites others to do the same, building trust and connection.

Getting Comfortable with Being Vulnerable

Start small. You don't have to pour out your soul to a new acquaintance. Begin by sharing your honest feelings or expressing uncertainty in a conversation. Say things like,

> *"I felt really nervous about that meeting,"*

or

> *"I'm not sure what the right answer is here."*

These honest admissions make you more relatable and human. The more you practice vulnerability, the more confident you'll become in your ability to connect authentically.

Creating a Safe Environment

To foster vulnerability in others, be a safe space. That means listening without judgment, validating their feelings, and respecting their boundaries. Respond with empathy and avoid giving unsolicited advice. When people feel emotionally safe with you, they're more likely to open up, deepening your bond.

Celebrating and Sustaining Meaningful Relationships

Acknowledging Milestones

Celebrating milestones—both big and small—reinforces the value of your relationships. Remember birthdays, anniversaries, or shared achievements. A thoughtful message or small gesture can go a long way in showing someone that you value them. These moments of recognition create emotional deposits that strengthen the foundation of your relationship.

Practices That Strengthen Connection

Meaningful relationships require intentional effort. Schedule regular time together, even if it's just a quick check-in. Create rituals, like weekly walks, monthly game nights, or an annual trip. These shared experiences deepen your sense of connection and create lasting memories. When life gets busy, these rituals act as anchors that keep the relationship strong.

Growing Together Over Time

Relationships, like people, evolve. Stay open to change. Have conversations about your goals, values, and needs as they shift. Practice gratitude—tell your loved ones what you appreciate about them. Reflect together on how your relationship has grown. These intentional moments foster a deeper sense of partnership and help your relationship adapt to life's inevitable changes.

Creating lasting connections isn't about being perfect—it's about being present, open, and emotionally attuned. When you bring emotional intelligence, trust, and vulnerability into your relationships, you give them the chance to deepen and thrive. These aren't one-time strategies—they're habits that, with time and intention, build bonds that can weather any storm.

Chapter 11: Key Takeaways

- **Emotional intelligence is the foundation of strong relationships** – develop self-awareness, empathy, and social skills to communicate with clarity and compassion.

- **Trust is built through consistency** – show up, speak honestly, and follow through on your word to strengthen relational bonds.

- **Vulnerability deepens connection** – being open about your feelings, imperfections, and fears invites authenticity and fosters emotional safety.

- **Meaningful relationships require maintenance** – celebrate milestones, create shared rituals, and check in regularly to sustain closeness.

- **Relationships grow with intentional reflection** – evolve together by discussing changing needs, expressing appreciation, and staying emotionally present.

Chapter 11: Practical Action Points

1. **Practice Emotional Intelligence**: Journal your emotional triggers and responses. Identify moments where you showed empathy or where you could have done better.

2. **Build Trust Through Communication**: Choose one relationship and commit to a weekly check-in. Focus on being open and honest in each conversation.

3. **Embrace Vulnerability**: Share something personal in your next conversation that reflects your authentic self.

4. **Celebrate Connection**: Plan a small celebration or appreciation gesture for someone important in your life.

5. **Reflect and Evolve**: Set a reminder each month to reflect on how your key relationships have grown and what they need to stay strong.

Talk Your Way to Success - Thriving at Work with Confident Communication

"Communication works for those who work at it."

\- John Powell

T he transition from school to the working world can feel like stepping into an entirely new universe—especially when it comes to communication. Entering the workplace for the first time can feel like a whole new world. The dynamics, expectations, and unwritten rules can be confusing—especially for young adults transitioning from academic life into professional environments.

Whether you're in your first internship, working remotely, or navigating office culture for the first time, the way you communicate can either build your reputation or quietly chip away at it. This chapter is here to help you confidently navigate workplace communication, from crafting professional emails to speaking up in meetings, and everything in between.

Let's explore the essential communication skills needed to thrive in the workplace—both in-person and digitally.

Understanding Workplace Communication

Workplace communication isn't just about sounding "professional" or using big words. It's about being clear, respectful, and reliable in your interactions. That means your tone, timing, and body language all work together to deliver a message that fits the context.

One major difference between casual and professional communication is intentionality. In the digital age, communication happens through a variety of channels: emails, Slack messages, Zoom calls, and collaborative tools like Google

Docs and Trello. Each platform has its own tone, pace, and etiquette. In casual chats, you might send a text full of emojis, or leave a message on read. But at work? Those same habits can come across as careless or even rude. For example, while a quick "Got it! " might be acceptable on Slack, the same message might come across as too casual in a formal email.

Professional communication values clarity and consideration, whether you're sending an email, jumping on Zoom, or leaving a Slack message.

Real-Life Scenario: Navigating Tone in Digital Messages

Here's a Scenario: You send your manager, let's call her Lucy, a quick Slack message saying, *"Did you finish the report yet?"* with no emoji or context. Your manager replies curtly, and the vibe feels... tense.

The Resolution: Consider how tone can be interpreted without voice or facial expressions. A better version is:

> *"Hi Lucy, just checking in—do you need any help wrapping up the report? Happy to pitch in if needed ⬚ "*

This softens the tone and offers support instead of pressure.

I've been guilty of this myself, especially when I'm in a rush. I quickly send a message and get straight to the point, not thinking about how the other person might interpret it. This is because in my head, I had nothing but good intentions but the person I'm sending it to might be having a bad day or something and take my message the wrong way. I often use to think, that's not my problem how they take things I say.

Especially if they take it the wrong way, but it's all part of growing as a person. I learned through experience that words have the power to profoundly change someone's life and once said and heard, you cannot take them back. No matter how badly you want to.

Key Takeaway: Digital tone matters. Adding context and warmth can prevent misunderstandings.

Even the platforms you use send signals. An email feels more formal than a chat message. A direct Slack ping may be urgent, while a message in a group thread might be less so. Learning how to match your message to the medium is one of the most important skills you can develop early on in your career.

Email, Chat, and Message Etiquette

Let's talk email first. Your subject line should be clear and concise, like a headline. Your opening should include a greeting, and your body should be broken into short, readable sections. Use bullet points if necessary, and always close with a sign-off and your name.

Here's a quick structure to follow:

- **Subject & Action Required**: Weekly Report Due Friday

- **Greeting**: *"Hi Jordan"*,

- **Body**: Keep it clear and to the point.

- **Close**: Best, [Your Name]

Avoid passive-aggressive phrases like *"per my last email"*—it might feel satisfying to say, but it can erode trust quickly. Instead, try,

> **"Just circling back to make sure you saw this"**

or

> **"Wanted to check in on the status of..."**

When using chat platforms like Slack or Microsoft Teams, treat messages as mini-conversations. Start with context, avoid dumping large blocks of text, and clarify expectations. For example:

> **Hey Sam! Quick question: do you have time to review the report draft today, or would tomorrow work better?**

This sounds friendly, gets to the point, and invites collaboration.

I'll be honest, I really struggle with this one, even to this day. I write large blocks of text to explain myself, thinking it will avoid confusion but it really just ends up giving myself more work. I'm actively trying to improve this skills daily.

Emails are the professional currency of communication. They should be clear, polite, and purposeful. Here are a few do's and don't to remember:

Do's:

- Start with a greeting ("Hi [Name],")

- State your purpose early

- Use bullet points for clarity

- Sign off professionally ("Best regards," "Thanks again," etc.)

Don'ts:

- Use slang or emojis

- Send long, unstructured paragraphs

- CC the entire office unless necessary

> **Pro Tip**: Always reread your emails before sending. Grammarly or spellcheck tools can catch mistakes, but your tone and clarity are up to you.

Video Calls and Virtual Meetings

With the rise of hybrid and remote work environments, virtual meeting etiquette is no longer optional—it's essential. Remote work is here to stay, and with it comes video meetings, which have their own set of unspoken rules.

Your professionalism on camera reflects your engagement and respect for the team.

Before the Meeting:

- Check your tech. Make sure your microphone, camera, and internet connection are working.

- Choose a quiet, well-lit space with a neutral background.

- Dress appropriately. Business casual is usually a safe bet—even if it's just from the waist up.

During the Meeting:

- Be punctual. Arrive a few minutes early to settle in and be ready.

- **Turn your camera on** (unless otherwise noted by your team culture) to show presence and engagement.

- **Look into the camera** when speaking to simulate eye contact.

- **Mute yourself** when not speaking to avoid background noise.

- **Use reactions or nodding** to show you're actively listening.

After the Meeting:

- Follow up with any promised documents or tasks.

- Send a thank-you or recap email if it was a one-on-one or important call.

Visual Etiquette Checklist:

- ☐ Tech working and background clean

- ☑ Camera on, face centered and well-lit

- ☑ Mic muted when not speaking

- ☑ No eating, texting, or side conversations

- ☑ Focused and contributing

Digital communication, especially on video, can feel impersonal, but small gestures of engagement can help you stand out for the right reasons. Mastering virtual presence shows you value your team's time and attention.

Setting Boundaries Professionally

It's tempting to always be available, especially in remote or hybrid roles where visibility can be limited. But setting boundaries is essential for protecting your well-being and doing your best work.

Use your calendar to block off lunch breaks or focus hours. Turn off notifications after work if your company respects off-hours boundaries. You can even include availability hours in your email signature:

> **Office Hours: Mon-Fri, 9:00am–5:30pm (EST)**

If a colleague sends a late message, it's okay to wait until morning to reply. You can even say:

> *"Thanks for the message! Following up this morning so I could give it proper attention."*

Giving and Receiving Feedback

Feedback is an essential part of professional growth, but it can feel uncomfortable to give or receive. One effective approach is using "I" statements and focusing on specific behaviors rather than personality traits. This strategy reduces defensiveness and invites constructive dialogue (Stone, Patton, & Heen, 2010).

Instead of:

 "You were confusing in the presentation."

Try:

> **"I had a hard time following the part about X—could you clarify it further next time?"**

This framing shifts the focus from blame to understanding, making feedback easier to give and more likely to be received well. When receiving feedback, listen fully before responding. Ask clarifying questions if needed. You don't have to agree with everything, but staying open will help you grow.

Building Professional Relationships

Good workplace relationships are built on respect, clarity, and follow-through. Whether you're collaborating on a project or attending team meetings, how you engage with colleagues makes a difference. Remember people's names, show appreciation, and be willing to help others.

These small gestures build trust and camaraderie.

When you're new to a job, don't be afraid to ask questions. Showing curiosity is not a sign of incompetence—it demonstrates a desire to learn and grow. Just be sure to do a bit of research first so you're asking informed questions.

Resolving Workplace Conflicts with Maturity

Conflict is inevitable in any professional setting, but your response can either escalate the issue or open the door to resolution. Mature conflict resolution is about addressing issues directly, clearly, and calmly—with the goal of mutual understanding, not blame.

Common Conflict Example: Imagine you're in a team meeting, and a co-worker presents a project update that includes your work but fails to mention your contributions. You're left feeling invisible and unappreciated.

What NOT to Do: Don't storm out, gossip with co-workers, or send a passive-aggressive email. These reactions might feel momentarily satisfying but damage your reputation and the work environment.

How to Respond:

- Ask your co-worker for a private conversation at a calm time.

- Instead of lashing out or venting to other colleagues, request a private conversation.

Try saying like:

> *"Hey, during the meeting today, I noticed my role in the project wasn't mentioned. I worked hard on X and Y, and I'd really appreciate being acknowledged in future updates."*

Why This Works: You're not accusing or attacking—you're using respectful, honest communication to express your feelings and ask for a change moving forward. This approach opens the door to resolution without escalating tension.

Visual Tip:

Conflict Resolution using Marshall Rosenberg's **'O.F.N.R.' Formula:**

1 | Observe – State the facts without judgment.

> "In today's meeting, I noticed my part in the presentation wasn't mentioned."

2 | Feel – Express your emotional response.

> "It made me feel overlooked and a little discouraged."

3 | Need – Clarify your underlying need.

> "I value being recognized for my work and contributions."

4 | Request – Make a clear, actionable request.

> "In future meetings, could we make sure everyone's contributions are acknowledged?"

This method, inspired by Nonviolent Communication (NVC), keeps things factual and avoids blaming. Using this approach builds trust and professionalism. It helps others understand your perspective while keeping the tone constructive and open.

Managing Up: Communicating with Your Boss

"Managing up" means making your boss's life easier while also advocating for your own growth and boundaries. According to Harvard Business Review, managing up involves anticipating your manager's needs, communicating proactively, and creating a partnership built on clarity and mutual respect (Hill & Lineback, 2011).

- **Keep them informed** – Don't wait for them to ask for updates—offer them.

- **Be proactive** – Anticipate problems and suggest solutions.

- **Set boundaries** – If your boss messages you outside of hours, it's okay to wait until the next workday to respond—unless it's urgent.

Real-Life Example: Your manager constantly assigns last-minute tasks at 4:45 PM.

What to Say:

"Hey Lucy, I want to do my best on each task. Could we set time earlier in the day to go over urgent priorities? That way I can allocate time effectively."

> **Takeaway**: You're expressing your need without blaming—and offering a solution.

Your Digital Presence is Your Reputation

One thing young professionals often underestimate is how digital footprints affect their workplace reputation. Everything you post online—even in private DMs or deleted posts—can resurface. According to CareerBuilder (2018), 70% of employers screen candidates' social media profiles during the hiring process. Employers check public profiles, Google candidates, and form opinions based on what they find.

Think twice before ranting about your boss or subtweeting your coworker. Before you hit send, ask: *"Would I be okay with my manager seeing this on a projector screen at work?"* If not, it might be worth rethinking.

Social media isn't off-limits, though. It can be a great way to build your professional brand—just be intentional. Share your passions, projects, and progress. Keep the tone you want to be known for.

Remember, **the internet is forever**. Screenshots exist, archive tools exist, and deleted doesn't always mean gone. So curate your digital presence with the same care you would your in-person image.

Workplace communication is one of the most important skills you'll ever develop—and the digital age makes it both more challenging and more rewarding. From resolving conflicts with confidence to adapting your tone across platforms, strong communication helps you build trust, grow professionally, and feel empowered at work. Start practicing these strategies today, and you'll stand out for all the right reasons.

Your Mini-Motto:

The workplace isn't just where you work. It's where you grow. Speak clearly. Type kindly. Listen fully. Reflect often.

WORDS THAT BUILD TRUST
UPGRADE YOUR WORK COMMUNICATION IN SECONDS

Avoid Saying		Say This
Just deal with it.	1	Let's discuss the obstacles and seek a solution.
That's not my responsibility.	2	I may not be the point of contact, but I can direct you to whom you need.
Here's how things are done here.	3	I'm receptive to new ideas – what do you have in mind?
I don't see an issue.	4	Help me comprehend what's not working for you.
I don't have time for this.	5	Let's allocate the appropriate time for time.
This isn't a top priority.	6	Let's reassess priorities and adjust accordingly.
You'll need to ask someone else.	7	While I can't determine that, I can provide my opinion.
That's just not possible.	8	Let's explore the variable options given our constraints.
You don't see my perspective.	9	Our views may not match – let me clarify.
This seems pointless.	10	What value does this add to our objective?
I'm indifferent to the outcome.	11	Let's decide on a strategy that suits all involved.
It's always like this.	12	If there are more efficient methods, let's dive into them.
You're blowing this out of proportion.	13	Please help me grasp your perspective- can you explain further?
That's how it's going to be.	14	Let's review this to resolve any uncertainties.

Chapter 12: Key Takeaways

- **Professional communication is intentional and respectful** – whether you're writing an email, sending a Slack message, or joining a Zoom call, tone and clarity matter.

- **Match your message to the medium** – different platforms require different levels of formality. Context is key.

- **Email, chat, and meetings each have etiquette rules** – keep emails concise and polite, chat messages collaborative, and video calls focused and professional.

- **Boundaries protect your well-being** – set clear working hours and communicate availability with confidence.

- **Feedback and conflict resolution require emotional maturity** – use respectful language, stay solution-focused, and lean into tough conversations with care.

- **Managing up is a power skill** – keep your boss informed, set realistic expectations, and offer proactive solutions.

- **Your digital footprint matters** – curate your online presence to reflect your personal brand, and always assume that what you post could be seen at work.

TALK YOUR WAY TO SUCCESS!

Chapter 12: Practical Action Points

1. Scan to Download the **Words That Build Trust Guide**

2. **Audit Your Digital Footprint**: Google yourself. Clean up any old posts or photos that don't reflect who you are now.

3. **Practice Writing Clear Emails**: Choose one email a day to rewrite before you send it. Focus on clarity, tone, and structure.

4. **Observe a Meeting**: Watch how seasoned professionals interact in meetings. Note their body language, word choice, and how they give feedback.

5. **Role-play Feedback**: Practice giving and receiving feedback with a friend. Use "I" statements and focus on solutions.

6. **Set Tech Boundaries**: Choose times each day to unplug from work messages. Let your team know and model healthy digital habits.

Growth Mode: On - Reflect, Learn, and Keep Leveling Up

"We do not learn from experience... we learn from reflecting on experience."

- John Dewey

There's something powerful about taking a moment to pause and look inward. In a world that's always pushing us to do more, say more, and be more, reflection is the tool that lets us slow down just enough to ask: How am I really doing?

In the journey of becoming a better communicator, self-reflection isn't just helpful—it's essential. It helps you recognize where you've grown, what's holding you back, and what to focus on next.

And one of the most accessible, powerful tools for self-reflection is journaling.

Journaling for Communication Growth

Understand the Purpose of Journaling

Journaling is more than a place to vent or recap your day—it's a mirror that helps you see your communication habits clearly. According to research by Burton and King (2004), expressive writing can reduce stress and improve emotional processing, both of which are vital for effective communication. Writing down your interactions helps you understand patterns, emotions, and challenges that might otherwise go unnoticed.

When you journal about a conversation, a meeting, or a public speaking experience, you start to see trends. Maybe you realize you interrupt more than you thought. Or perhaps you notice that certain people make you nervous, which affects your tone. Over time, journaling becomes a personal growth tracker that shows how far you've come—and where there's room for improvement.

Techniques for Effective Journaling

To make journaling impactful, you need structure. Start by setting a regular time to write—maybe at the end of each day or after important conversations. Use specific prompts like:

- What communication situation stood out today?

- What went well?

- What could I have done differently?

- How did I feel before, during, and after?

- What did I learn about myself?

You don't need to write a novel — just a few honest lines. This consistent reflection sharpens your self-awareness and builds emotional intelligence.

According to Daniel Goleman (1995), emotional intelligence includes five core components—self-awareness, self-regulation, motivation, empathy, and social skills—which are widely recognized as predictors of personal and professional success.

Using Journals to Identify Strengths and Weaknesses

Once journaling becomes a habit, you can use it to spot communication strengths and areas for growth. Flip through past entries and highlight recurring themes. Are you confident in one-on-one conversations but freeze in groups? Do you often misunderstand others' tones in text messages? Your journal becomes a personalized feedback system.

From there, set improvement goals based on what you discover. Maybe your goal is to ask more open-ended questions or to maintain eye contact during conversations. Journaling helps you track these goals, adjust them, and celebrate your wins.

Incorporating Journaling into Daily Routine

To stay consistent, pair journaling with an existing habit. Maybe you write in your journal after brushing your teeth or right before bed. If you prefer digital tools, apps like Day One or Journey offer reminders and voice-to-text features.

Even if you're short on time, a 5-minute journal entry is enough to make a difference. It's not about quantity—it's about quality and consistency. By carving out a few minutes each day, you commit to becoming more intentional and self-aware.

Setting and Achieving Communication Goals

The Importance of Clear Communication Goals

Setting clear goals gives your communication growth a direction. Instead of vaguely wanting to "get better at talking to people," a specific goal might be: "Speak up once in every group meeting this month." That's measurable, realistic, and focused.

Extensive research on goal-setting shows that specific, written goals are more likely to lead to motivation, commitment, and success (Locke & Latham, 2002). Goals help break big changes into manageable steps, keeping you motivated and accountable.

Developing a Goal-Setting Framework

Use the SMART framework to create your communication goals:

- **Specific** – Define the exact skill you want to improve.

- **Measurable** – Identify how you'll track your progress.

- **Achievable** – Make sure the goal is realistic for your current skill level.

- **Relevant** – Align the goal with your values and needs.

- **Time-bound** – Set a deadline to stay on track.

For example: "Initiate a conversation with one new person every week for the next month." This goal is clear, doable, and meaningful.

Strategies for Achieving Communication Goals

To stay on track, share your goals with someone you trust—an accountability buddy or mentor. Set calendar reminders or use habit-tracking apps like Habitica or Notion. Visualize yourself succeeding and reflect on progress weekly. These small actions compound over time and keep you moving forward.

Evaluating and Adjusting Goals

Growth isn't linear. Sometimes, life shifts or a strategy doesn't work. That's okay. Schedule monthly check-ins to assess your goals:

- Am I making progress?

- What's working?

- What needs to change?

Adjust your goals as needed—this shows adaptability, not failure. For example, if a goal feels too hard, break it into smaller steps. If it's too easy, raise the bar.

Learning from Feedback and Criticism

Embracing Feedback as a Growth Opportunity

Feedback is one of the fastest ways to grow—but only if you're open to it. Constructive criticism offers insights you might not see on your own. Instead of viewing feedback as a personal attack, reframe it as a chance to level up.

Research by Stone and Heen (2014) shows that receiving feedback well is a skill in itself—one that involves emotional regulation, curiosity, and resilience. When someone offers feedback, take a breath and ask yourself,

What can I learn from this?

Techniques for Receiving Feedback Gracefully

- **Listen fully** before responding. Don't interrupt or get defensive.

- **Ask clarifying questions:** "Can you give an example?"

- **Thank the person** for their input.

- **Reflect before reacting**—sit with the feedback before making changes.

These strategies create space for growth and show emotional maturity.

Turning Feedback into Actionable Insights

Not all feedback is equally useful. Learn to filter the noise. Focus on feedback that's specific, behavior-based, and actionable. For example, "You always talk over people" is vague, but "Try pausing before responding" is helpful.

Once you understand the message, turn it into a mini-goal: "Pause for two seconds before replying in meetings." Track your efforts in your journal and adjust as needed.

Seeking and Offering Constructive Feedback

Growth-minded people don't wait for feedback—they ask for it. After a presentation or conversation, try: "Was there anything I could've communicated more clearly?" This opens the door for honest insights.

Equally important is learning how to give feedback. Keep it kind, specific, and focused on behavior, not personality. Use the "sandwich method": positive – suggestion – positive.

Fostering a feedback-positive environment helps everyone grow. It creates a culture of openness and mutual respect.

Adapting to Changing Social Dynamics

Recognizing Evolving Social Norms

The way we communicate is constantly changing—especially in the digital age. What worked five years ago might feel out of touch now. Think about how emojis, video calls, and voice notes have shifted our communication habits. Staying aware of these changes helps you stay relevant and respectful.

Different generations communicate differently, too. Gen Z often favors quick texts and memes, while older generations might prefer emails or phone calls.

Understanding these nuances helps you adapt your approach based on who you're talking to.

Strategies for Flexibility and Adaptability

To build adaptability:

- Practice communicating with different types of people—online and offline.

- Reflect on your assumptions and how they affect your tone.

- Be willing to adjust your language, formality, or platform to match the context.

Adaptability doesn't mean changing who you are. It means learning how to meet others where they are—without losing your voice.

Embracing Change as a Learning Opportunity

Change isn't always comfortable, but it's always an opportunity to grow. When social dynamics shift—whether through culture, technology, or trends—ask yourself:

- What's new about this situation?

- What can I learn here?

- How can I improve the way I respond?

Write these reflections in your journal. Treat each change as a training ground for stronger communication.

Cultivating a Growth Mindset

At the heart of all this is mindset. People with a growth mindset believe they can improve through effort, learning, and persistence. Carol Dweck's research (2006) shows that this mindset leads to greater resilience and achievement.

When it comes to communication, a growth mindset helps you:

See awkward moments as learning experiences

Approach challenges with curiosity instead of fear

Stay open to feedback and change

It's not about being perfect. It's about being better than yesterday. And that starts with choosing growth—one small, consistent step at a time.

Self-reflection and continuous growth are the heartbeat of powerful communication. They turn everyday experiences into lessons, and feedback into fuel. Whether you're journaling your interactions, setting and achieving specific goals, or adapting to changing social dynamics, the journey is ongoing.

The more aware and intentional you become, the stronger and more confident your communication skills will be.

Remember, this isn't about perfection—it's about progress.

Embrace your growth, celebrate your small wins, and keep showing up with curiosity, courage, and an open mind. Because communication is more than what we say—it's how we show up, listen, learn, and grow.

Chapter 13: Key Takeaways

- **Self-reflection is the foundation of communication growth** – journaling about your interactions reveals patterns, progress, and areas for improvement.

- **Consistent journaling builds emotional intelligence** – even five minutes a day sharpens self-awareness and helps you communicate more effectively.

- **Set SMART communication goals** – specific, measurable objectives give your growth direction and make success trackable.

- **Embrace feedback as fuel** – responding with openness and turning criticism into actionable steps accelerates your development.

- **Adapt to social and digital shifts** – communication styles evolve with culture and technology; stay flexible to remain effective and relevant.

- **Cultivate a growth mindset** – see awkward moments, mistakes, and challenges as opportunities to improve, not as failures.

- **Communication isn't a destination – it's a journey** – the more you reflect, adjust, and stay curious, the more confident and capable you become.

Chapter 13: Practical Action Points

1. **Start a Communication Journal**: Use daily prompts to reflect on conversations and interactions. Keep it brief but consistent.

2. **Set a SMART Goal**: Choose one communication habit to improve and apply the SMART criteria.

3. **Seek Feedback**: Ask a trusted peer or mentor for honest feedback on your communication style.

4. **Track Progress**: Use your journal to document wins, challenges, and adjustments.

5. **Embrace Change**: Identify one recent social shift and explore how you can adapt your communication approach to fit it.

Your Online Voice - Crafting a Personal Brand that Speaks for You

"Your brand is what other people say about you when you're not in the room."

- Commonly attributed to Jeff Bezos

L et's be real: in today's world, your online presence is your reputation. It's your resume, your character reference, and your first impression—all rolled into one. Whether you're applying for a job, meeting someone new, or collaborating on a project, the first thing people often do is Google your name. What comes up can either open doors or close them.

In this chapter, we're going to talk about why digital reputation matters, how to manage it wisely, and how to build a personal brand that reflects who you truly are.

Your Digital Footprint Is Forever

Here's the thing: the moment you post something online—a comment, a photo, a video, or a story—you leave a digital trace. Many people underestimate how long their personal data remains online. Even deleted posts can often be retrieved through screenshots, caches, or archived (Kaspersky, 2022). What you post today in a moment of frustration or fun could resurface years later in an entirely different context.

We're not saying you can never have fun or be yourself online. But we are saying that being intentional about what you share is powerful. You are in control of how you show up digitally. Think of every post, tweet, or story as a piece of your personal brand.

Ask yourself:

> **"Would I be okay with a future employer, mentor, or partner seeing this?"**

If the answer is no, reconsider hitting publish, or if you've already published it consider deleting.

Curating a Digital Identity That Aligns with Your Values

Your digital presence should reflect the real you—your interests, goals, personality, and values. It doesn't have to be polished to perfection, but it should be authentic. Start by auditing your current social media profiles. What do your bios, photos, and posts say about you?

Would someone looking at your profile get a sense of what you care about and what you bring to the table?

Building a personal brand isn't just for influencers or entrepreneurs. Everyone has a personal brand, whether you're intentional about it or not. Your brand is how people perceive you based on what you consistently share and how you engage.

If you want to be known as someone who's creative, reliable, and insightful, make sure your posts reflect that. Share your thoughts on topics you care about. Highlight your wins and lessons. Support causes that matter to you.

Digital Etiquette: Be Thoughtful, Not Performative

Engagement matters. The way you comment, repost, or respond to others online says a lot about your character. Are you kind and respectful, even when you disagree? Do you uplift others, give credit, and acknowledge different perspectives? Practicing good digital etiquette builds credibility and trust.

Avoid performative actions—those that are done just to be seen as supportive or "on trend." People can tell when you're being disingenuous. Instead, be intentional. Speak on what matters to you, not what everyone else is posting just to stay relevant. In the long run, sincerity stands out more than virality.

Avoiding the Pitfalls of Oversharing

Social media can create pressure to share everything. But not every moment needs to be public. Oversharing can blur the lines between personal and professional, and not everyone needs access to every detail of your life.

If you're someone who uses social media as a journal or venting space, consider using a private journal or talking to a trusted friend instead. Emotional outbursts online may feel cathartic in the moment but can cause damage to your image or relationships. Remember, the internet doesn't forget.

A good rule of thumb: Post with intention, not impulse.

Reputation Recovery: What to Do If You Mess Up Online

Mistakes happen. Maybe you posted something without thinking, or someone dug up an old post that doesn't reflect who you are today. First, take accountability. Don't delete and deny—acknowledge what happened, apologize sincerely, and explain how you've grown.

Reputation recovery takes time, but it's possible. Be consistent in showing who you are now. Use your platforms to demonstrate your growth and values. People appreciate transparency and change more than perfection.

Your digital presence is powerful. It tells the story of who you are, who you were, and who you're becoming. Don't leave that story up to chance. Take control of it. Be intentional. Be proud of it. And remember—once it's out there, it's out there for good.

So let your digital legacy be one that future you will thank you for.

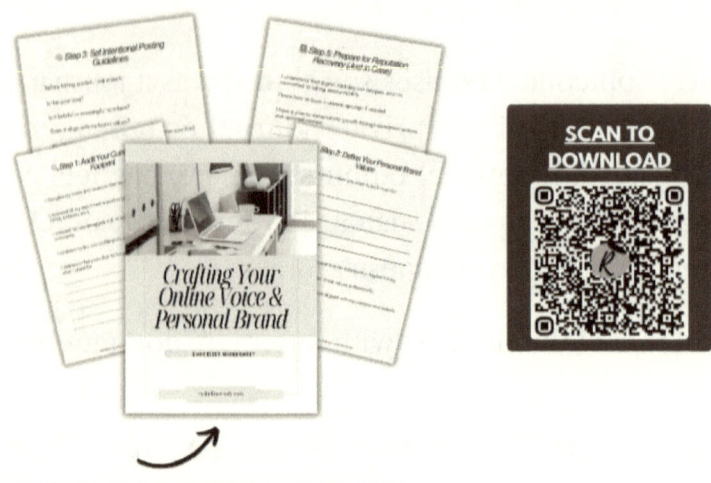

CREATE A PERSONAL BRAND YOU LOVE!

Chapter 14: Key Takeaways

- **Your digital footprint is permanent**—every post, comment, and share shapes your online reputation, even if deleted later.

- **Your personal brand already exists**—being intentional allows you to align it with your real values, goals, and personality.

- **Authenticity over perfection**—share content that reflects who you truly are, not who you think others expect you to be.

- **Digital etiquette matters**—be respectful, thoughtful, and sincere in online interactions; performative behavior erodes trust.

- **Avoid oversharing**—post with purpose, not impulse, and

protect the parts of your life that deserve privacy.

- **Mistakes don't define you**—acknowledge, grow, and move forward; consistent positive actions rebuild credibility over time.

Chapter 14: Practical Action Points

1. **Audit Your Digital Presence**: Scan to Download the **Personal Brand Checklist Workbook** and Google yourself and review all your social media profiles. What kind of impression would someone form from your digital footprint?

2. **Clean Up Old Content**: Remove or hide posts that no longer represent who you are. Update bios and photos to reflect your current goals and personality.

3. **Clarify Your Brand Values**: Identify 3-5 values or traits you want to be known for (e.g., creativity, leadership, empathy) and start reflecting them in your posts and interactions.

4. **Set Posting Guidelines**: Create a personal checklist to review before you post. Ask yourself: Is this helpful? Is it kind? Does it align with my values?

5. **Practice Digital Boundaries**: Choose what you want to keep private. Consider having separate accounts for personal and professional life, and manage privacy settings intentionally.

Dating with Clarity - Navigating Online Romance with Confidence

"Don't trade your authenticity for approval."

- Brené Brown

Let's talk about something real—dating in the digital age. For young adults, apps like Tinder, Bumble, Hinge, and even Instagram DMs have replaced the classic coffee shop meet-cute.

And while online dating opens up a world of possibilities, it also brings a unique set of challenges.

This chapter is all about helping you approach online dating with confidence, clarity, and boundaries, so your experiences are empowering—not exhausting.

Understanding the Landscape of Online Dating

Online dating can feel like a fast-paced game. Swipe right. Swipe left. Match. Ghost. Repeat. It's easy to get caught up in the cycle without really thinking about what you're looking for or how you're presenting yourself.

Here's the truth: dating apps are tools. How you use them matters. According to Pew Research Center (2019), 48% of adults ages 18–29 have used a dating site or app. Of those, many reported both positive and negative experiences. The key? Being intentional.

Start by asking yourself what you're really looking for—casual conversation, friendship, dating, or something long-term. Your clarity helps you set boundaries, avoid mismatched expectations, and recognize red flags sooner.

Crafting an Authentic Dating Profile

Your dating profile is like your personal billboard. It introduces you before you even speak. But you don't have to be perfect—you just have to be real.

Here are some tips:

- **Choose photos that reflect who you are**—not just flattering angles. Show real-life moments doing what you enjoy: hiking, gaming, creating, exploring.

- **Write a bio in your own voice.** Use humor if that's your thing, and be upfront about your intentions.

- **Avoid exaggeration.** Pretending to be someone else won't sustain a real connection.

> **Remember:** you don't need to appeal to everyone. You just need to be seen by the right people.

Setting Boundaries Early

Just because you're swiping and chatting doesn't mean you owe anyone your time, energy, or emotional availability. Setting boundaries is your right.

Some boundaries to consider:

- **Time boundaries**: Don't feel pressured to respond immediately or stay up chatting all night.

- **Privacy boundaries**: Don't share your address, full name, or personal routines early on.

- **Emotional boundaries**: You're not obligated to share your full life story with someone you just matched with.

If someone ignores or challenges your boundaries, that's a red flag. Respect is the foundation of any healthy connection.

Navigating Conversations with Intention

Texting on apps can feel shallow—but it doesn't have to be. Try starting with questions that go beyond "Hey."

Instead of:

> **"What's up?"**

Try:

> **"What's something that made you laugh this week?"**, **"If you could instantly master any skill, what would it be?"**

These types of questions spark deeper dialogue. They also help you get a feel for someone's values, humor, and personality.

Pay attention to the flow of the conversation. Do they ask questions back? Do they respect your responses? Are they pushing your boundaries? These clues can tell you a lot.

Recognizing Red Flags and Trusting Your Gut

In online dating, not every connection will be healthy. Here are some common red flags to watch out for:

- Love-bombing early on: Over-the-top affection before trust is built

- Avoiding personal details or video calls

- Guilt-tripping when you set boundaries

- Trying to rush into a relationship or meet-up

Listen to your gut. If something feels off, it probably is. Your intuition is a valid form of data. Block, unmatch, or report when necessary. Your safety matters more than being polite.

Meeting in Person Safely

If things are going well and you decide to meet IRL (in real life), follow these safety steps:

- **Meet in a public place** for the first few dates.

- **Tell a friend where you're going** and who you're meeting. Ping your friend your location.

- **Keep your phone charged** and trust your instincts – leave if you feel uncomfortable.

- **Avoid sharing your home address early on.**

- **Avoid getting into a date's vehicle on the first meeting** to stay in control of your surroundings.

You deserve to feel safe and respected at every stage of connection. Never compromise that for the sake of chemistry.

Online Dating and Emotional Wellness

Online dating can take a toll on your self-esteem if you're not mindful. Ghosting, rejection, or endless swiping can make you question your worth. Here's your reminder: your value isn't determined by matches, replies, or relationship status.

Studies have shown that dating apps can contribute to emotional fatigue, especially when rejection or superficial matches become the norm. If you're feeling depleted, it's a sign to step back, reset, and reconnect with yourself offline.

Dating in the digital age doesn't have to be overwhelming or confusing. With the right mindset, boundaries, and tools, you can build meaningful connections while protecting your peace. Be clear, be kind, and most of all—be yourself. The right person will appreciate exactly who that is.

Until then, honor your boundaries, take care of your peace, and remember—you're already whole.

Chapter 15: Key Takeaways

- **Online dating is a tool—how you use it matters.** Approach it with intention and clarity about your goals and values.

- **Authenticity attracts alignment** – curate your dating profile to reflect your real self, not a highlight reel or a persona.

- **Boundaries are non-negotiable** – set and enforce limits around time, privacy, and emotional energy from the start.

- **Conversation quality matters** – ask intentional questions that spark genuine connection and reveal shared values.

- **Watch for red flags** – listen to your intuition and exit conversations that feel disrespectful, manipulative, or unsafe.

- **Prioritize safety when meeting IRL** – public meetups, check-ins with friends, and trusting your instincts are key.

- **Protect your emotional health** – ghosting and rejection aren't reflections of your worth. Take breaks when needed and date from a place of fullness, not depletion.

NAVIGATING ONLINE DATING WITH CONFIDENCE

CRAFT AN AUTHENTIC PROFILE

- Use genuine photos
- Write an honest bio

SET CLEAR BOUNDARIES

- Don't feel obligated to chat constantly
- Guard your personal info
- Share at your own pace

WATCH FOR RED FLAGS

- Love-bombing
- Disrespect for boundaries
- Rushing into commitment

PRIORITIZE SAFETY

- Meet in public places
- Tell someone your plans
- Trust your instincts

Dating should enhance your life, not deplete it.

Chapter 15: Practical Action Points

1. **Clarify Your Intentions**: What are you looking for in online dating? Define your purpose before you download the app.

2. **Set Profile Standards**: Choose photos and write a bio that represents the real you.

3. **Establish Boundaries**: Make a mental list of what you're comfortable sharing and what's off-limits.

4. **Craft Conversation Starters**: Save a few intentional openers to use instead of "Hey."

5. **Plan Safe Meetups**: Have a plan in place for meeting someone in real life. Don't skip safety steps.

6. **Schedule Wellness Breaks**: If you feel drained, take a break. Your emotional well-being matters.

Safe, Smart, and Seen - Protecting Yourself in a Digital World

"It takes 20 years to build a reputation and five minutes to ruin it."

- As Warren Buffett famously said

L iving in a digital age means more than just knowing how to communicate online—it means knowing how to protect yourself too. As we navigate an increasingly connected world, we open ourselves up to incredible opportunities... but also potential risks. That's why understanding digital safety, managing your online privacy, and learning how to recognize and respond to red flags is essential for anyone who wants to build smart, lasting relationships online.

Whether you're sliding into DMs, joining new communities, or networking professionally, this chapter is your guide to protecting your peace.

Understanding the Importance of Online Safety

Being active online doesn't mean being vulnerable. But many young adults overlook basic safety steps because they assume only "sketchy" platforms pose a risk. The truth? Even the most legitimate apps and platforms can become unsafe if you don't manage your digital footprint wisely.

According to Pew Research Center (2022), 41% of young adults between 18–24 have experienced online harassment. This includes unwanted contact, cyberstalking, and exposure to inappropriate content. The takeaway? Protecting yourself isn't about paranoia; it's about preparation. Make online safety part of your communication strategy, just like you would with face-to-face interactions.

Red Flags to Watch For in Online Interactions

When you meet someone online, especially on social media or dating platforms, pay close attention to their behavior and how they make you feel. Here are some common red flags to look out for:

- **Overly persistent or pushy behavior**: If someone pressures you to reply quickly or share personal details, that's a warning sign.

- **Avoiding video chats or in-person meetings**: Especially if you've been talking for a while. People who avoid showing their face may be hiding something.

- **Inconsistent stories or evasiveness**: If their background, work, or location keeps changing, something's off.

- **Love-bombing early on**: Extreme praise and emotional intimacy from someone you barely know can be manipulative.

- **Requests for money or personal information**: No matter how convincing the story, never send money to someone you've never met in person.

Trust your gut. If something feels weird, it probably is. Don't hesitate to block, report, or remove yourself from the situation.

Keeping Your Personal Information Private

Your full name, address, phone number, workplace, and even daily routines can be used to identify and manipulate you. That's why it's crucial to:

- Limit the information you share publicly on social media.

- Be cautious when sharing your location.

- Use secure, strong passwords and enable two-factor authentication.

- Avoid clicking on suspicious links, even from people you know (accounts get hacked too).

Make it a rule: if you wouldn't share it with a stranger in real life, don't post it online.

Spotting Catfishing and Scams

Catfishing—when someone pretends to be someone else online—is still a real threat, especially in romantic and social settings. Common tactics include using fake photos, impersonating someone with a glamorous lifestyle, or emotionally manipulating you to gain your trust.

Romance scams are one of the fastest-growing categories of online fraud. In fact, according to a 2023 report by the Federal Trade Commission (FTC), nearly 70,000 people reported a romance scam, and reported losses hit a staggering $1.3 billion alone in the last year.

To protect yourself:

- Reverse-image search suspicious profile pictures.

- Ask for a video call early in your conversations.

- Never send personal photos, money, or sensitive information to people you haven't met.

Managing Digital Boundaries

Just like in real life, boundaries matter online. That means deciding what you're comfortable sharing, when you're available, and how you respond to pressure.

Set digital boundaries by:

- Turning off read receipts or setting "Do Not Disturb" during certain hours.

- Letting people know when you're unavailable to talk.

- Saying "no" clearly when someone oversteps.

Boundaries protect your mental and emotional well-being, especially in environments that move fast and demand constant connection.

Teaching Yourself to Pause Before You Post

Sometimes, the biggest safety risk comes from impulsive sharing. Whether it's venting in your stories or sharing personal struggles, it's easy to forget how public the internet really is. Once something is posted, it's out of your hands. Even deleted posts can leave a trail—screenshots, cached versions, and saved media don't disappear with a delete button.

Before posting something emotional, sensitive, or revealing, ask yourself:

- Am I okay with anyone seeing this 5 years from now?

- Would I want a potential employer or mentor to read this?

- Am I posting this to inform, or to seek validation?

If you're unsure, pause. Sleep on it. You can always choose to keep some things offline.

Your digital world should feel safe, empowering, and aligned with who you are. The more proactive you are in protecting your online space, the more confident and free you'll feel showing up as your full self—both online and off. Remember: safety and connection go hand in hand.

Chapter 16: Key Takeaways

- **Online safety is not optional—it's essential**. Protect your digital footprint with the same care you'd use to protect your physical identity.

- **Red flags matter**—trust your gut when you encounter behaviors like pushiness, evasiveness, love-bombing, or requests for money.

- **Privacy is power**—limit how much personal info (like location, workplace, or full name) you share online and use privacy tools like two-factor authentication.

- **Catfishing and scams are real threats**—verify identities early with video calls, reverse-image searches, and never send sensitive information or money.

- **Boundaries online are just as valid as offline**—set limits on when you're available and what kinds of interactions you'll tolerate.

- **Pause before you post**—protect your future self by

asking if today's post could affect tomorrow's reputation, safety, or emotional peace.

<u>Chapter 16: Practical Action Points</u>

1. **Audit Your Privacy Settings**: Check every app and platform you use. Update settings to limit what strangers can see or message.

2. **Memorize Online Red Flags**: Make a mental (or written) list of behaviors you won't tolerate in online interactions.

3. **Strengthen Your Passwords**: Use a password manager and update old passwords that are weak or reused.

4. **Set Digital Boundaries**: Decide when and how you want to be available online. Stick to those boundaries.

5. **Pause Before Posting**: Set a 10-minute buffer before sharing anything emotional or personal. Rethinking helps protect your future self.

CHAPTER 17
The Long Game - Becoming a Master Communicator for Life

"Do the best you can until you know better. Then when you know better, do better."

- Maya Angelou

If you've made it this far, congratulations. You've taken bold steps toward transforming how you show up in the world—and how the world responds to you. But here's the truth: great communicators aren't born, and they don't arrive at a final destination. Communication mastery is a lifelong journey. It grows with you as you move through different seasons of life—college, career, friendships, partnerships, parenthood, and everything in between.

This final chapter is your roadmap for what comes next.

Communication Is a Living Skill

Let's get real for a second. Most of us learned how to talk, but very few of us were ever taught how to truly communicate. We mimic what we see—parents arguing, influencers posting perfectly curated content, or TikTok creators delivering snappy advice. And while these all shape our style, genuine, confident, and conscious communication takes intentional practice.

Like working out, the gains come with consistency. You might master active listening one month, then realize a year later that you've been tuning people out again. That's okay. The key is noticing, adjusting, and continuing to grow.

Real-life Example:

Consider Zendaya, who has evolved her communication style over the years—from quiet Disney Channel interviews to now confidently leading conversations on race, culture, and representation in Hollywood. Her growth didn't happen overnight. It reflects ongoing effort, intention, and emotional intelligence.

Pop culture shows us this all the time. Look at Taylor Swift's public transformation—from the girl who kept quiet during controversies to someone who now controls her narrative, advocates for herself, and speaks on complex political issues. Or watch any season of *Queer Eye*, where communication becomes a powerful vehicle for healing, growth, and self-discovery.

These figures aren't perfect—they're evolving. And so are you.

The goal isn't flawless delivery; it's to keep leveling up your awareness, empathy, and ability to connect authentically.

Whether you're navigating a new workplace, setting boundaries in a romantic relationship, or making a first impression on a Zoom interview, your communication toolbox needs to evolve with you.

Whether you're navigating a new workplace, setting boundaries in a romantic relationship, or making a first impression on a Zoom interview, your communication toolbox needs to evolve with you.

A growth plan turns inspiration into action.

Create Your Communication Growth Plan

Let's turn this from a vibe into a vision. Building a communication growth plan gives you a practical way to keep applying what you've learned. Here's how to do it:

1. Reflect on Strengths & Challenges

- What do people often compliment you on? (Listening? Humor? Warmth?)

- What situations trigger your anxiety or cause miscommunication?

2. Set Intentional Goals

- Use the SMART method (Specific, Measurable, Achievable, Relevant, Time-bound).

- Examples: "I will initiate one meaningful conversation per week with someone I don't know well" or "I'll practice speaking up in meetings twice a month."

3. Track Your Progress

- Journal after conversations or keep a quick log of wins and learning moments.

- Use voice memos to reflect if you're not a fan of writing.

4. Expand Your Circle

- Follow creators, thinkers, and professionals who model the kind of communication you admire.

- Attend events, webinars, or online groups where you can practice new skills.

5. Revisit and Revise Every Season

- Life changes—and so will your communication needs. Reassess every few months.

Research on habit formation shows that small, consistent actions build long-term change.

30-Day Communication Challenge

Let's put it into practice. Try one of these every day for 30 days:

1. Compliment someone authentically.

2. Ask a stranger a curious, respectful question.

3. Say no to something that doesn't align with your values.

4. Send a thank-you message.

5. Practice a 1-minute elevator pitch.

6. Journal about your last uncomfortable conversation.

7. Reconnect with someone you've lost touch with.

8. Practice deep listening—no interrupting.

9. Leave a thoughtful comment on a creator's post.

10. Express vulnerability with a trusted friend.

(...and so on. Make your own list. Make it personal.)

Connection Is Your Superpower

If you take nothing else from this book, let it be this: communication is the bridge to every opportunity, every relationship, and every transformation you'll ever have. It's not about being perfect. It's about being present.

It's about making people feel seen, heard, and respected—and allowing yourself to be seen too.

Your voice matters. Your words matter. And your growth? It's just getting started.

Let this chapter be the beginning of your next one.

Chapter 17: Key Takeaways

- **Communication is a living skill**—not something you master once, but something you grow and refine throughout life's seasons.

- **Consistency beats perfection**—you'll slip up, unlearn, and relearn. What matters most is staying aware and adjusting along the way.

- **Your growth reflects intention**—like Zendaya or Taylor Swift, evolving communicators embrace authenticity, advocacy, and adaptability.

- **Build a communication growth plan**—reflect on your strengths and challenges, set SMART goals, and commit to regular self-check-ins.

- **Practice makes progress**—small daily actions (like

compliments, thank-yous, and honest conversations) compound into powerful transformation.

- **Connection is your superpower**—your ability to listen, speak truthfully, and show up authentically is what shapes your relationships and your future.

- **Your voice matters—and your journey is just beginning**—embrace the long game and keep leveling up with presence, purpose, and heart.

Inspire a New Young Adult to Learn About Communication!

Now you have everything you need to have effective, meaningful conversations, form strong bonds with people from all walks of life, and build lasting confidence. It's time to pass on your newfound knowledge and show other readers where they can find the same help.

Simply by leaving your honest opinion of this book, you'll show other young adults where they can find the information they're looking for, and pass their passion for learning how to level up their communication skills forward.

Feeling the love and don't want our journey together to end? Visit <https://roshelinarush.com> for more free, helpful content to help you level up your young adult life. I'm committed to helping you and others like you reach your personal goals.

Thank you so much for reading this book. Knowing that my message is reaching those who need it most means the world to me. I can't wait to hear about your success.

Thank you, from the bottom of my heart.

— Roshel Waite

Conclusion

Congratulations—you've made it to the final pages of a journey that could transform how you connect, express, and show up in your life.

This guide has been uniquely tailored for the digital era—where emojis, video calls, social media, and messaging apps are part of everyday connection.

From navigating online conversations with emotional intelligence to setting boundaries and building confidence, you've learned what it takes to communicate with clarity and purpose in a hyperconnected world.

Summing Up Your Journey

Throughout this book, you've explored the foundations of powerful communication. You've learned how to listen deeply, speak with authenticity, and respond with emotional awareness.

You've practiced tools like active listening, visualization, goal-setting, boundary-setting, and journaling to strengthen how you show up in every kind of interaction—from private chats to public platforms.

You didn't just read about communication—you began to live it.

Why Communication Still Reigns

Strong communication isn't optional. It's the foundation for every meaningful relationship, opportunity, and turning point in your life. It helps you:

- Express your ideas clearly

- Handle conflict with maturity

- Build trust, influence, and connection

Whether you're making friends, negotiating your salary, sending an email, or leading a meeting—how you communicate *is* how you lead.

Practical Tools That Stick

You've built a toolkit that works across real-life and digital spaces. These aren't just theories—they're tools you can use immediately:

- Journaling prompts to sharpen self-awareness

- SMART goals to direct your growth

- Templates for thank-you notes, boundary-setting, and conversations

- Scripts, questions, and cues to deepen everyday connection

Use them. Adapt them. Make them yours.

From Insight to Action

A growth plan turns inspiration into action.

Now it's time to commit to the next step.

Create Your Communication Growth Plan

Here's a simple way to stay intentional:

1. **Reflect**: What's already working for you? What challenges keep repeating?

2. **Set SMART Goals**: (Specific, Measurable, Achievable, Relevant, Time-bound). E.g., "I'll start one thoughtful conversation each week."

3. **Track Progress**: Use a journal, a voice note, or a checklist to keep tabs on wins and learning moments.

4. **Stay Inspired**: Follow people who model the kind of communication you admire.

5. **Check In Often**: Revisit your plan every few months. You're evolving—so should your goals.

Try a 30-Day Communication Challenge

Try something small every day:

- Compliment someone sincerely

- Say "no" with kindness

- Reach out to someone new

- Pause before replying when emotional

- Speak up once in a meeting or group

Little steps = lifelong growth.

Communication Is Your Superpower

You don't need to be perfect. You just need to be present. Every message, every gesture, every pause is a chance to connect, to grow, to lead.

Look at the growth of people like Zendaya—once a quiet presence in early interviews, now a powerful speaker on identity and culture. Or Taylor Swift, who shifted from silence to speaking boldly on ownership and politics. Communication evolves with you. Let it.

This isn't about being flawless. It's about showing up with heart.

What's Next?

Keep learning. Take a workshop. Join a community. Read more books like:

- *Emotional Intelligence 2.0* by Bradberry & Greaves

- *Crucial Conversations* by Patterson et al.

- *Thanks for the Feedback* by Stone & Heen

Growth-minded communicators never stop refining.

With presence and purpose,

Roshel Waite

You're ready. Go speak truth. Connect deeply. Advocate boldly.

This is just the beginning.

About the author

Roshel Waite is an internet entrepreneur, author, editor, and founder of a popular website (Roshel in a Rush - https://roshelinarush.com/).

Her website provides helpful information & resources on navigating the challenges of Young adulthood & Student life. She helps countless young adults achieve their personal, academic, and professional goals.

To find out more information about her books, visit her website at: https://roshelinarush.com/books

Check out other books by Roshel Waite

Helpful Resources

Do you want a full list of helpful resources to help you level-up your young adulthood and communication skills?

- **Roshel in a Rush – website**

  - <https://roshelinarush.com>

- **Resource Library**

  - <https://roshelinarush.com/free-resource-library/>

WEBSITES...

- **Roshel in a Rush – blog**

  - <https://roshelinarush.com/blog>

Scan the QR Code or Click the link to see the FULL list of helpful resources to complement this book.

Sources & References

American Psychological Association. (2023). Stress in America 2023: Young adults and social media. https://www.apa.org/news/press/releases/stress/2023/social-media-young-adults

Bodie, G. D., Worthington, D. L., & Gearhart, C. C. (2013). The listening styles profile-revised (LSP-R): *A scale revision and evidence for validity*. Communication Quarterly, 61(1), 72-90.

Brown, B. (2012). *Daring greatly: How the courage to be vulnerable transforms the way we live, love, parent, and lead.* Gotham Books.

Brooks, A. W. (2019). Breaking the Ice: The Importance of Small Talk. Harvard Business Review. Retrieved from https://hbr.org/2019/08/breaking-the-ice-the-importance-of-small-talk

Cain, S. (2013). *Quiet: The power of introverts in a world that can't stop talking.* Crown Publishers.

Doidge, N. (2007). T*he brain that changes itself.* Penguin Books.

Doran, G. T. (1981). *There's a S.M.A.R.T. way to write management's goals and objectives. Management Review,* 70(11), 35-36.

Hill, L. A., & Lineback, K. (2011). Being the boss: The 3 imperatives for becoming a great leader. Harvard Business Review Press.

Iacoboni, M. (2009). *Mirroring people: The science of empathy and how we connect with others.* Picador.

Kabat-Zinn, J. (2013). *Full catastrophe living: Using the wisdom of your body and mind to face stress, pain, and illness.* Bantam Books.

Healthline. (2022). Affirmations for Anxiety: How to Make and

Use Them. Retrieved from https://www.healthline.com/health/mental-health/affirmations -for-anxiety

Lehrman, L. (2010). Churchill, Hitler, and "The Unnecessary War": How Britain Lost Its Empire and the West Lost the World. *Journal of Historical Review*, 9(1), 1-12.

Mehrabian, A. (1971). *Silent messages*. Wadsworth Publishing.

BetterHelp. (n.d.). Positive Visualization: The Scientific Benefits Of Visualization. Retrieved from https://www.betterhelp.com/advice/visualization/positive-visu alization-the-scientific-benefits-of-visualization/

Calm. (n.d.). Suffering from social media overload? 7 tips to help you cope. Retrieved from https://www.calm.com/blog/social-media-overload

Perry, A. (2021). Why Authentic Communication Matters. LinkedIn. Retrieved from https://www.linkedin.com/pulse/why-authentic-communicati on-matters-alexis-perry

Resilience Lab. (n.d.). Digital Overload: Read This If Your Screen Time Is Out of Hand. Retrieved from https://www.resiliencelab.us/thought-lab/digital-overload

Berkowitz, S. (2012). The importance of icebreakers in group communication. International Journal of Medical Education, 3, 76–77. https://doi.org/10.5116/ijme.4f91.2f54

Bruess, C. (2022, July 21). Why Curiosity in Conversations Is Key to a Healthy Relationship. Wit & Delight. https://witanddelight.com/2022/07/curiosity-in-conversations -healthy-relationship

Lammers, J., & Gast, A. (2017). How humor makes you more influential. Stanford Graduate School of Business Insights. https://www.gsb.stanford.edu/insights/make-em-laugh-how-h

umor-can-be-secret-weapon-your-communication

The Financial Times. (2023, October 11). The power of silence in conversations. Financial Times. https://www.ft.com/content/a058df24-22bf-4537-b171-2da604efcdc6

Kidd, D. C., & Castano, E. (2013). Reading literary fiction improves theory of mind. Science, 342(6156), 377–380. https://doi.org/10.1126/science.1239918

Brownell, J. (2012). Listening: Attitudes, Principles, and Skills (5th ed.). Pearson.

Decety, J., & Jackson, P. L. (2006). A social–neuroscience perspective on empathy. Current Directions in Psychological Science, 15(2), 54–58. https://doi.org/10.1111/j.0963-7214.2006.00406.x

Goleman, D. (1995). Emotional intelligence: Why it can matter more than IQ. Bantam Books.

Cvijikj, I. P., & Michahelles, F. (2013). Online engagement factors on Facebook brand pages. Social Network Analysis and Mining, 3(4), 843–861. https://doi.org/10.1007/s13278-013-0098-8

Derks, D., Fischer, A. H., & Bos, A. E. (2008). The role of emotion in computer-mediated communication: A review. Computers in Human Behavior, 24(3), 766–785. https://doi.org/10.1016/j.chb.2007.04.004

Ganster, T., Eimler, S. C., & Krämer, N. C. (2012). Same but different!? The differential influence of smilies and emoticons on sender's and receiver's perception of social presence. Computers in Human Behavior, 28(5), 187–191. https://doi.org/10.1016/j.chb.2011.08.007

Kalyanaraman, S., & Sundar, S. S. (2006). The psychological appeal of personalized content in web portals: Does customization affect attitudes and behavior? Journal of Communication, 56(1), 110–132. https://doi.org/10.1111/j.1460-2466.2006.00006.x

Kushlev, K., & Dunn, E. W. (2015). Checking email less frequently reduces stress. Computers in Human Behavior, 43, 220–228. https://doi.org/10.1016/j.chb.2014.11.005

Betancourt, J. R., Green, A. R., Carrillo, J. E., & Ananeh-Firempong, O. (2003). Defining cultural competence: A practical framework for addressing racial/ethnic disparities in health and health care. Public Health Reports, 118(4), 293–302. https://doi.org/10.1016/S0033-3549(04)50253-4

Chung, R. C., Bemak, F., Ortiz, D. P., & Sandoval-Perez, P. A. (2016). Promoting the mental health of immigrants: A multicultural/social justice perspective. Journal of Counseling & Development, 94(3), 298–306. https://doi.org/10.1002/jcad.12086

Greenwald, A. G., McGhee, D. E., & Schwartz, J. L. K. (2009). Measuring individual differences in implicit cognition: The implicit association test. Journal of Personality and Social Psychology, 74(6), 1464–1480. https://doi.org/10.1037/0022-3514.74.6.1464

Gudykunst, W. B. (2004). Bridging differences: Effective intergroup communication (4th ed.). Sage Publications.

Page, S. E. (2007). The difference: How the power of diversity creates better groups, firms, schools, and societies. Princeton University Press.

Bandura, A. (1997). Self-efficacy: The exercise of control. W.H. Freeman.

Goldin, P. R., & Gross, J. J. (2010). Effects of mindfulness-based stress reduction (MBSR) on emotion regulation in social anxiety disorder. Emotion, 10(1), 83–91. https://doi.org/10.1037/a0018441

Holmes, E. A., & Mathews, A. (2010). Mental imagery in emotion and emotional disorders. Clinical Psychology Review, 30(3), 349–362. https://doi.org/10.1016/j.cpr.2010.01.001

Porges, S. W. (2011). The polyvagal theory: Neurophysiological foundations of emotions, attachment, communication, and self-regulation. W.W. Norton & Company.

Mehrabian, A. (1972). Nonverbal communication. Aldine-Atherton.

Taylor, S. E., & Pham, L. B. (1996). Why thinking about goals and processes improves performance: A social cognitive perspective. Psychological Review, 103(3), 403–409. https://doi.org/10.1037/0033-295X.103.3.403

Zak, P. J. (2014). Why your brain loves good storytelling. Harvard Business Review. https://hbr.org/2014/10/why-your-brain-loves-good-storytelling

Gottman, J. M., & Gottman, J. S. (2015). The seven principles for making marriage work: A practical guide from the country's foremost relationship expert. Harmony Books.

Mayo Clinic. (2024). Assertive communication: Tips for being assertive. Retrieved from https://www.mayoclinic.org/healthy-lifestyle/adult-health/in-depth/assertive/art-20044644

Apollo Technical. (2023). 40+ Networking Statistics for 2023. https://www.apollotechnical.com/networking-statistics/

Granovetter, M. (1995). Getting a Job: A Study of Contacts and Careers (2nd ed.). University of Chicago Press.

Jobvite. (2022). Recruiter Nation Report. https://www.jobvite.com/

LinkedIn. (2016). Relationships matter. https://news.linkedin.com/2016/10/relationships-matter

LinkedIn. (2018). Networking and Follow-Up Best Practices. https://business.linkedin.com/

LinkedIn Marketing Solutions. (2021). The LinkedIn Guide to Content Marketing. https://business.linkedin.com/marketing-solutions/blog

Locke, E. A., & Latham, G. P. (2002). Building a practically useful theory of goal setting and task motivation: A 35-year odyssey. American Psychologist, 57(9), 705–717. https://doi.org/10.1037/0003-066X.57.9.705

Burton, C. M., & King, L. A. (2004). The health benefits of writing about intensely positive experiences. Journal of Research in Personality, 38(2), 150–163. https://doi.org/10.1016/S0092-6566(03)00058-8

Dweck, C. S. (2006). Mindset: The new psychology of success. Random House.

Goleman, D. (1995). Emotional Intelligence: Why it can matter more than IQ. Bantam Books.

Stone, D., & Heen, S. (2014). Thanks for the Feedback: The science and art of receiving feedback well. Penguin Books.

Stone, D., Patton, B., & Heen, S. (2010). Difficult conversations: How to discuss what matters most (2nd ed.). Penguin Books.

Speed, B. C., Goldstein, B. L., & Goldfried, M. R. (2018). Assertiveness training: A forgotten evidence-based treatment. *Clinical Psychology: Science and Practice*, 25(1), e12216. https://doi.org/10.1111/cpsp.12216

Brackett, M. A., Warner, R. M., & Bosco, J. S. (2006). Emotional intelligence and relationship quality among couples. Personal Relationships, 12(2), 197–212.

Brown, B. (2012). Daring greatly: How the courage to be vulnerable transforms the way we live, love, parent, and lead. Gotham Books.

Goleman, D. (1995). Emotional Intelligence: Why It Can Matter More Than IQ. Bantam Books.

Goleman, D. (2006). Social Intelligence: The New Science of Human Relationships. Bantam.

Kaspersky. (2022). Digital Amnesia: A Growing Threat to Today's Online Generation. Retrieved from https://www.kaspersky.com

Kaspersky. (2022). Digital reputation and privacy: Survey results. [R e p o r t] . https://www.kaspersky.com/blog/digital-reputation-privacy-re port/

Walther, J. B., & Parks, M. R. (2002). Cues filtered out, cues filtered in: Computer-mediated communication and relationships. In Handbook of Interpersonal Communication (pp. 529–545). Sage Publications.

Federal Trade Commission. (2023). Romance scammers' favorite lies exposed. https://www.ftc.gov

Pew Research Center. (2022). The State of Online Harassment. https://www.pewresearch.org

Livingstone, S., & Helsper, E. J. (2007). Gradations in digital inclusion: Children, young people and the digital divide. New Media & Society, 9(4), 671–696.

Pew Research Center. (2020). The Virtues and Downsides of Online Dating. https://www.pewresearch.org

LeFebvre, L. E. (2018). Swiping me off my feet: Explicating relationship initiation on Tinder. Journal of Social and Personal Relationships, 35(9), 1205–1229.

Ansari, A., & Klinenberg, E. (2015). Modern Romance. Penguin Press.

Goleman, D. (2006). Social Intelligence: The New Science of Human Relationships. Bantam.

Rosenberg, M. B. (2003). Nonviolent Communication: A Language of Life. PuddleDancer Press.

CareerBuilder. (2018). The State of Workplace Communication Survey. Retrieved from https://press.careerbuilder.com

Harvard Business Review. (2021). Digital Body Language: How to Build Trust and Connection, No Matter the Distance by Erica Dhawan.

Dhawan, E. (2021). Digital Body Language: How to Build Trust and Connection, No Matter the Distance. St. Martin's Press.

Brown, B. (2012). Daring Greatly: How the Courage to Be Vulnerable Transforms the Way We Live, Love, Parent, and Lead. Gotham Books.

Goleman, D. (1995). Emotional Intelligence: Why It Can Matter More Than IQ. Bantam Books.

Clear, J. (2018). Atomic Habits: An Easy & Proven Way to Build Good Habits & Break Bad Ones. Avery.

Dweck, C. S. (2006). Mindset: The New Psychology of Success. Random House.

Harvard Business Review. (2020). Why Soft Skills Matter. Retrieved from https://hbr.org